I confess: I'm a *huge* fan of gadgets. But I al
pull up at the touch of a finger can lead to discontent and distractions. This is a topic
that's been on Doug Smith's heart for a long time. And the biblical advice he provides
in *UnIntentional* is spot-on.

— **DAVE RAMSEY**, Best-selling author and nationally syndicated radio show host

UnIntentional addresses one of the core issues that is contributing to our nation's
loss of ability to think critically. Doug Smith is a seasoned learner, practitioner and
expert in the disease of media addiction in our screen-saturated world. Doug's heart
and passion is to help people recognize this undiagnosed addiction in their own
lives, and to provide principles and practical insights for overcoming the disease.
UnIntentional is a must read for anyone with a computer, smart phone, or television.

— **TODD WILSON**, Founder and Director of Exponential,
author of *More: Find Your Calling and Live Life to the Fullest Measure*

No topic is more critical in our screen-saturated culture. For any parent, for any
grandparent, for any individual living with the constant distractions of this reality
in their daily lives, this book comes as a beautifully-crafted and grace-filled invitation to manage the noise, to prioritize well, and to pay attention to the things in
life that are significantly more important than one's Instagram account. Thank you,
Doug, for sounding a clarion call to intentional living.

— **MICHAEL A. VANDER KLIPP**, Editor-at-Large,
HarperCollins Christian Publishing | Zondervan

It is easy to live unintentionally: swept along by currents of materialism, consum-
erism and empty philosophy that pervade our world through electronic media. For
those of us who want to live life more intentionally, Doug Smith's book provides the
biblical insights and mental tools needed to glorify God in a world that aims to enslave our minds. Finally, I've found the book I need for myself, my family and friends.

— **TIMOTHY J. BARNETT**, PhD, Professor of Political Science,
author of *America's False Recovery*

This practical, insightful, and engaging book will help families navigate the media
world today. I recommend it enthusiastically to everyone who wants to be intentional about developing great relationships.

— **QUENTIN SCHULTZE**, PhD, Professor of Communication Emeritus, Calvin College,
author of *Habits of the High-Tech Heart: Living Virtuously in the Information Age*

UnIntentional has the feel of a modern Christian classic, a rare gem of a book for those
of us now swimming in a screen crazed world—carefully researched yet written in such
an engaging and honest style that it's difficult to put down. After reading Doug's book, I
found myself feeling a new courage to live this life to the full, with the tools and knowledge to avoid the snares that so often drag us down into the tepid and mediocre life. This is
not just a book for the West, but a book that's relevant for those of us throughout the world
who are trying to live as God *intended*!

— **MATTHEW CONNOR**, International Scripture Arts Consultant,
Wycliffe Bible Translators

Wow, what an engaging book! Doug Smith offers a piercing description of how Satan uses technology to negatively influence our lives and subtly draw us into immorality. But he also offers hope and a bold vision for how to overcome the challenge of our technology driven lives. This book is a stirring call to faithfully put God first in our daily lives and put technology to the periphery where it belongs.

— **DR. BOBBY HARRINGTON**, Lead Pastor and Executive Director, Discipleship.org

What an important book for our time! With the kind of clarity that normally comes only with hindsight, Doug helps us get a glimpse of ourselves, and our culture, during this age of extreme transition. You should read this book!

— **ANDY HUDELSON**, Senior Pastor, WellSpring Christian Church

Doug Smith has done his homework. This book is an amazing and diligent collection of facts telling how our culture has been influenced by our media screens. Doug skillfully implements biblical principles and practices with very practical solutions to overcome and replace the addictions that are so prevalent. Doug's experience with the technical world as well as his own victory over addictions has made him well qualified to broach this topic.

As a pastor for over 35 years, I highly recommend that other pastors share this book with their parishioners, or use it as a counseling resource to help those dealing with addictions in their congregations. It should be an annual read for all pastors.

— **REV. MARK BODENSTAB**, Pastor, Church of the Nazarene

Doug Smith has been providentially appointed to shed light on the dark and deceptive practices of our world's media empires! Pulling back the hidden veil of their intentional tactics to keep God's people from achieving their calling and purpose in life, Doug reveals Truth that will set you free to accomplish all that God intended for you to achieve. For His Glory!

— **DAN BANKS**, President and CEO, 9Fruits LLC

Doug's book draws much needed awareness to a problem that has remained blind to most people. His experience with technology, coupled with his mastery of the written word, makes this a *must* read for us all. He gives practical advice that enables you to liberate your time and your mind from years of being held hostage.

— **LANCE WESTBROOKS**, M.S., Associate Professor, Middle Tennessee State University

Congratulations on the book! I am delighted to be an endorser of your work; it sounds like a very timely topic! Your experience with technology combined with your God-driven sense of ministry will no doubt produce a product that blesses and brings healing to those who struggle.

— **EDWARD FUDGE**, Pastor, Theologian, Lawyer, author of *The Fire That Consumes*

[UN]INTENTIONAL

DOUG SMITH

[UN]INTENTIONAL

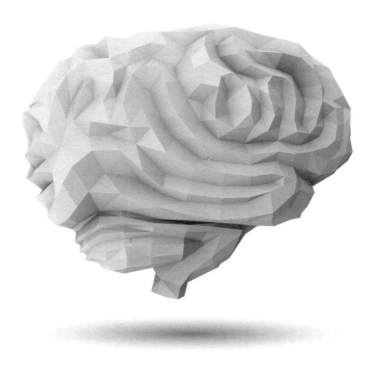

HOW SCREENS SECRETLY SHAPE YOUR DESIRES
AND HOW YOU CAN BREAK FREE

credo
house publishers

Editing by Michael A. Vander Klipp
Front cover design by Christopher Carrico
Interior design by Sharon VanLoozenoord
Back cover photo by Samantha Johnson, Monumental Moments Photography

CONTENTS

For Stephanie, Tiffany, Mariah, Katie,
and all of your families to come

■ ■ ■

May you all live in intentional freedom,
by the grace God gives to us all

[UN]INVITED

AN INTRODUCTION TO *[UN]INTENTIONAL*

I'm proud of you. You've started a book designed to help you live a life of intentional freedom in today's screen-saturated world. You may feel the tentacles of technology wrapping around the throats of everyone you know, and you are hoping there's help—somewhere. Just the act of starting a book like this is a huge step in the right direction.

Early test readers found this book surprising, challenging, inspiring, and life-changing. But when they read the first few chapters, some of them felt unsettled. One said, "this scares the Cheez Whiz out of me." Another compared it to that part in *The Matrix* where Neo is offered a red pill or a blue pill, which means either a chance to see the world as it really is, or go back into blissful ignorance. That reader knew if he kept reading, he'd be exposed to hidden realities about the world—and about himself—and he wasn't sure he was ready.

But these readers kept going, found tremendous hope, and are already enjoying the benefits of applying what they've learned.

In this brief introduction, my goal is to assure you that if you push through the parts that may "scare the Cheese Whiz" out of you, it will be worth it. To that end, here's a quick look at the overall structure of the book.

First, the chapter titles. Like the book's title *[Un]Intentional*, each chapter title describes a negative character trait that has applied to each of us at some time in our lives. Each chapter will help you drop the "Un" and develop the positive character trait that remains. For example, instead of being *[Un]aware* or *[Un]prepared*, you'll be more *aware* or *prepared* than ever. Ultimately, the book will lead you to erase the "Un" from *[Un]Intentional* on a journey toward the intentional life you were made to live.

The twelve chapters of the book fall loosely into three sections: *Awaken*, *Examine*, and *Overcome*.

Chapters 1–4 will **awaken** you to what screen immersion is doing to us, expose specific techniques and strategies used to manipulate us, introduce the people and companies behind these intentionally addictive technologies, then reveal the spiritual dimension that underlies it all. It's a cumulative case that may be a little uncomfortable at times. But I know you'll be grateful for the wake-up call because of the value you'll find later.

Chapters 5–6 encourage you to **examine** your life in light of what you've learned. As you begin to evaluate where you are, I think you'll be relieved by the gracious tone of what I call "postures of evaluation." From there, you'll be encouraged to envision and anticipate what your life could be like if no harmful influences were holding you back.

The last section of the book teaches you how to **overcome** by applying five biblical practices. These practices have helped me to live in more freedom than I've ever known, even as distractions and obsessive technologies have multiplied exponentially. We'll finish with an inspiring call to embrace and apply all you've learned, both for your good and the good of those who need you to overcome.

May I encourage you: fasten your seatbelt if you need to, but read the whole book. If you feel challenged, or even a little frightened in the beginning, please don't give up. In fact, if you want to overcome fear, giving up is the last thing to do, because the biblical practices I share in the final chapters are infused with fear-destroying hope.

Right now, you are living the only life you have been given. This is your chance. And it's not over. In fact, no matter where you are right now—even if you feel far behind where you had hoped to be at this point in your life—you're just getting started. The rest of your life is ahead of you, and there is hope—more hope than you may be able to imagine right now.

Let me repeat: I'm proud of you. Proud that you are willing to consider a book like this one. If you'll read this book and adopt the practices I share, I'm confident that you will experience more freedom than you've ever known. I want that for you.

Guess what? You've already dropped one "Un." Now, you're *invited* to finish *[Un]Intentional.*

CHAPTER 1

[UN]AWARE

WHAT OUR SCREEN-SATURATED WORLD IS DOING TO YOU

Reality

What if everything you know—or think you know—is contrived? Scripted? Designed to keep you playing along, and you're unaware? How would you know?

Truman Burbank had no idea he'd lived his entire life as the star of the TV phenomenon that shared his name: *The Truman Show*. As the first baby ever adopted by a corporation, Truman's world included fake parents, a manufactured childhood, and a marriage to an actress who only pretended to be his wife. Only when cracks in the façade became apparent—a spotlight fell from the fake sky, a car radio accidentally broadcast cues of his movements, and a fake elevator revealed a hidden room—did Truman begin to question the authenticity of everything he had ever known.

Back in our real world, the whole planet is being turned into a reality show, and the "directors" keep the "cast members" of the world on script through the devices we carry in our pockets and the screens on every wall. The scenario played out in the movie is all too real today. Most people are like Truman before things start falling apart—unaware of what's happening. They play their appointed roles, cued by desire-manufacturing technologies that lead them to often unfortunate destinations.

And eventually the façade begins to show itself for what it is through the havoc it creates: broken relationships, addictions, and the sense of missing the lives we were made to live.

What's Happening?

If someone swerves on the interstate in front of you, what's your first thought? More often than not, you see their head as you pass them, turned down in that telltale way, the familiar bluish glow illuminating their distracted face.

Have you ever had someone walk into you with their head down, hypnotized by the glow? Have you ever entered a crowded, yet silent room, with everyone immobilized as if under a powerful spell? What about walking by those families at the restaurant, nobody saying a word to each other because it's like they were zapped by a freeze ray from an old B-grade sci-fi movie? You know what they're all doing.

The statistics are unbelievable.

In May 2017, eMarketer found the average US adult will spend over twelve hours a day consuming media on devices like smartphones, computers, and TVs.[1] We achieve that staggering twelve-hour figure by multitasking, like watching TV while scrolling Facebook. Six of those daily hours are spent on our smartphones, tablets, or laptops.[2] During our daily media smorgasbord, we are seeing between 4,000-10,000 ads per day.[3] In about the minute it will take you to read this paragraph, in the US alone another seven million videos will be watched on Snapchat; Instagram users will like over two-and-a-half million posts; and three-and-a-half million text messages will be sent.[4]

The eMarketer study also claimed our media consumption is plateauing at the twelve-hour daily average, so the acceleration of our consumption over the past decade is tapering off. It seems like we're reaching a saturation point, becoming fully immersed with no more non-work time to spend consuming media on our screens. (Remember, that twelve-hour number is the *average*: some do less, and some do much more.)

Reed Hastings, CEO of Netflix, declared that his company's primary competition is not Amazon or YouTube, but *sleep*. According to *The Guardian*, Hastings said, "You know, think about it, when you watch a show from Netflix and you get addicted to it, you stay up late at night. We're competing with sleep, on the margin. And so, it's a very large pool of time."[5] You heard him right. For Netflix to continue to grow long-term, they've got to entice us to sleep less and binge watch more. Notice the CEO of Netflix *wants* us to "get addicted." And addicted we are.

We're just starting to learn the negative impact of devices on our sleep. Not only are we sleeping less, but the quality of our sleep is also decreasing because of our devices. The blue spectrum of light from a screen makes us feel as if it's daytime even during the night. Plus, the vibrant flashiness of the media we consume keeps our brains active, anxious, and distracted well after we finally close our eyes. Lower-quality sleep is impacting our bodies in multiple ways: from weakening our immune systems, to producing heart disease, high blood pressure and diabetes, to generating mental health disorders and even impairing fertility.[6]

In a February 2017 article titled "Tech Ate the Media and Our Minds,"[7] Jim VandeHei and Sara Fischer say, "our brains have been literally swamped and reprogrammed" by our immersion in billions of daily tweets, Facebook messages, videos, and web page views. Because of this explosion of content, media companies have made a "deal with the devil to dumb things down (and lose credibility) by seeking the broadest reach." And while 62% of US adults get their news on social media, 68% don't trust what they watch or read. All of us are rightly skeptical (e.g. "fake news"), but where are we being led? If we're "swamped and reprogrammed" by increasingly foolish content, how can we expect to have the brain power to address the really important issues of our age?

The Change

It's hard to remember, but we weren't always so immersed in technology. When I was born in 1966, my family had one black & white

TV—the kind with a dial, three channels, and a rabbit-ear antenna that I played with and broke. (Sorry, Mom.) By the time I was in high school in the early 80s, we had a couple of color televisions in the house and cable, a VCR, and a ColecoVision game console. We were an average middle-class suburban family in Northeast Portland, Oregon, so most of my friends had similar technology. With the birth of the personal computer in the late 80s and early 90s, we saw new screens show up in homes, and in the late 90s, those screens started connecting to the new-born internet with the screech of modems connecting to phone lines.

From the seed of those first televisions, a carnivorous, all-consuming vine has wrapped its tentacles around every corner of our lives. Nearly everyone has seen its fruit, with multiple screens in every room of every house, every restaurant, every church, and almost every pocket or purse across much of the globe. We are entangled.

And the world has never seen such a rapid or impactful change. The iPhone is only just over a decade old. At over 1.2 Billion (1,200,000,000) units sold (as of August 2017), it's the most successful product of any kind ever made.[8] Analyst Horace Dediu summarizes iPhone's overwhelming victory, saying, "It unleashed forces which we are barely able to perceive, let alone control. It changed the world because it changed us." He's right. Everyone—from babies who hold a pacifier in one hand and an iPhone in the other, to the most aged former technophobes—is being reshaped by our screen-saturated world.

Future sociologists will study this time in human history and have 20/20 hindsight to accurately assess the real impact of today's screen immersion on humanity. But as we live through this era in real time, the tragic fact is that we're largely unaware of how this technology has fundamentally changed the way we live, work, and interact with others. And that should make us concerned.

But why should we be concerned, you might ask? What's the big deal? Aren't the amazing new capabilities and connections changing everything for the better?

How do we know whether anything is good or bad, anyway?

Jesus said we can "know a tree by its fruit." Good fruit comes from good trees, and bad fruit . . . well, you know. What fruit is growing from the crop of screens we have planted?

Known by the Fruit

We've heard stories and probably even know people who are on the extreme end of the negative technology impact spectrum: the brilliant young men who spend their formative decades addicted to video games; the young girls tricked into sending pornographic selfies; and the marriages destroyed by Tinder. Almost daily, a new and extreme case of technology-enabled insanity captures our attention in the news.

But most people feel the impact in less apparent ways. Surrounded by devices supposedly intended to connect us, we instead feel lonely as our loved ones embrace their devices rather than us. Even when we are engaged in real-time conversation, we often glance at our phones, as distraction is just a fingerprint scan away. We argue with our kids about their time on devices, and we fight to protect them from ever-lurking and ever-deepening online dangers.

When I got my first smartphone in 2010, I quickly felt myself pulled by the device like a compass needle to a magnet. The power of constant connection was intoxicating. Before I realized what was happening, I almost physically craved new notifications of emails, updates, or instant messages.

Soon, I felt habitually compelled to check the device for something, anything new. Before I realized it, I was reading email from my bed as my first half-dazed action of the day, and I ended every night falling asleep on Twitter. I also saw family, friends, co-workers, neighbors and strangers all captivated by their new handheld companions. It started feeling like we had been infected by a dangerous virus of epidemic proportions.

If I couldn't sit still for five minutes without looking for something new on this device, then what was happening to my ability to have a coherent, original thought? If the content of nearly every spare moment was prioritized by this device's agenda, where was I being led? And if my entire family was becoming absorbed with devices instead of talking or reading or moving, what would happen to our most important relationships?

What if our very ability to think clearly, and therefore, to be ourselves, was at stake?

As a web developer, I knew how it all worked, and I was conflicted.

As a lifelong admirer of new technology, part of me was fascinated. I was amazed at the phenomenal technical achievement represented by the supercomputer in my pocket. On the other hand, I felt we (I and society in general) were losing something important. By becoming engulfed in constant messages through our screens, we were changing, and it wasn't an upgrade.

Concerning Downgrades

People are talking a lot about screen-catalyzed consequences these days, so I know they'll be familiar to you. Here are brief comments on five of my biggest concerns.

Distraction

The reality of this is obvious. We can't go anywhere—*anywhere*—without seeing someone staring at a device unless we're staring at our own. When we look up from our screen, there's another screen in front of us—on the wall, the gas pump, or the digital billboard.

But it's not just that we're distracted. We *have to* be distracted. We don't know how to be quiet in our own thoughts, or even pause for a breath between activities. We've become compulsively impatient. The increasing speed of our pocket supercomputers makes us expect speed in every other arena of life. Never fear—anytime we have to wait, our phone is always near to make any inconvenient delay bearable. Boredom, that fertilizer of creativity, is choked to death.

Uncivil Discourse

The coarsening of conversation on social media is a modern cliché. We all know people who are instantly ignited to anger, often saying things online they'd never say to another person face-to-face. With their inhibitions dropped, they're primed and ready to be offended at a keyword. Say the wrong thing, and BOOM, you'll hear about it, often from a tirade laced with profanity.

I know people who were lifelong friends before the 2016 election cycle. Because of increasingly uncivil discourse, they had to unfriend or mute their former BFFs because of the constant barrage of political diatribes. Our online incivility prevents us from having productive conversations that could move things forward, even with those who—unthinkably—hold different views from our own.

Mocking

You don't have to scroll long before you see some group being mocked by another. Mocking has almost become a worship style on TV, with stand-up comics and talk show hosts competing for the biggest laugh at the expense of those on the other side. You're hateful, bigoted, anti-science, stupid, or maybe even evil or wicked if you hold views different from what is being made mainstream.

The constancy of mocking is nearly habitual, so many people's initial response to anything is to ridicule it on social media. And while mocking is as old as the Bible, technology has weaponized modern scoffing. Unfortunately, tech-powered scornfulness is crippling society's ability to make positive change.

Sexualization

One of today's most popular TV shows is HBO's *Game of Thrones*. Tens of millions of people are binge-watching season after season of what is essentially violent pornography. Normalizing and esteeming shows like *Game of Thrones* in our culture does not reduce the harmful effect on our hearts and minds.

The top music, movies, and commercials are frequently hyper-sexualized. As a dad to four daughters, I find society's pornified view of women to be directly opposed to who I want my girls to become. The screen-powered message of culture to young women and girls is that they need to look, dress, and act salaciously in order to be valuable.

Deep Thought Impossible

The insidious result of these societal downgrades is the near-elimination of clear thinking. Without the ability to think deeply, we lose our capacity to evaluate what is really going on around us. If we're always distracted, consuming more uncivil, ridicule-filled, and sexualized content, we'll be unable to take a step back, see a fresh perspective, and do something beneficial.

One of my biggest fears is that, drowning in screens, we'll lose the desire to think deeply at all. We'll be so immersed and satisfied with all of our media that we'll just accept it as the inevitable result of "progress." We'll even become advocates for the continual degradation of humanity, as long as the media continues to fill our minds with more pleasing entertainment.

Worse for the Young?

The negative effect of screen time on young people is a serious concern.[9] Of course, we're upset by the reports of increasingly early exposure to pornography (with a heartbreaking average first exposure anywhere between eight and eleven years old),[10] the cyber bullying, and drug-like addictive online behaviors. And beyond those larger issues lies the degradation of basic social skills. Have you ever tried to interact with kids who are so immersed in their screens that they can't participate in a verbal conversation? Or who are becoming so disconnected from flesh-and-blood reality that they are losing their empathy? The reduction of real-time, undistracted human interaction is taking a significant toll on our youth.

Once thought to be a savior ready to rescue struggling students, technology in the classroom may actually harm our kids' ability to learn. Dr. Nicolas Kardaras, author of *Glow Kids: How Screen Addiction is Hijacking Our Kids—and How to Break the Trance*, said in a 2016 *Time* article that "Screens in schools are a $60 billion hoax."[11] Giant tech companies have pushed laptops and tablets as a panacea for learning, but it isn't working, Kardaras says. "Tech in the classroom not only leads to worse educational outcomes for kids, it can also clinically hurt them."[12] His survey of the literature shows that "over two hundred peer-reviewed studies point to screen time correlating to increased ADHD,[13] screen addiction,[14] increased aggression,[15] depression,[16] anxiety[17] and even psychosis."[18] Dr. Ryuta Kawashima agrees, saying, "It's no exaggeration to say that kids today are being controlled by smartphones, and becoming enslaved by them."[19]

The negative impact of mobile devices on kids has become so troubling there's even a petition in Colorado to ban smartphones from children under thirteen.[20] The initiator, Dr. Tim Farnum, was shocked by the dramatic changes in his eleven and thirteen-year-old sons when they were given their first smartphones. The article says, "his once-energetic and outgoing boys became moody, quiet, and reclusive." When he tried to take away the phones, "one of Farnum's sons launched into a temper tantrum that the dad described as equivalent to the withdrawals of a crack addict." I know young people who exhibit this same behavior.

Bringing it Home

How about you? You probably picked up this book because you recognize the possibility that screens are negatively affecting some part of your life. You may have family members who are showing addictive behaviors or who are constantly distracted by their screens. If you have kids, you and your children may be on opposite sides of a tug-of-war, with some screen or another in the middle.

So, how are you navigating today's screen-saturated world? Do you find yourself waking up and going to sleep with your glowing companion, staring hypnotically at faces in an online book, a blue bird, or your friends' snappy chats? Is your time watching Netflix or playing video games growing while the dreams you had for your life are fading away? Or, are you stuck in more harmful behaviors like viewing pornography, online gambling, or compulsive gaming? Is your job, your family, or even your health suffering?

How about your relationship with God? Do you sense a distance, or find yourself wondering if he's there at all? Do you remember a time when your faith was vibrant, but now you rarely have time for prayer, Bible reading, or listening for his voice? Do you remember feeling a call on your life when you first believed, but today, your higher calling feels distant and impractical?

I've been there. I was a casualty of the cultural scourge of pornography, caught up in temptations that threatened to destroy everything I loved. I've also lived a life of anxious activity, driven by an electronic taskmaster. By God's grace and with a practiced intentionality empowered by him, I've been transformed to the place where, miraculously, I'm writing this book and sharing what I've learned with you.

That's why I want to help you find your way to the life you were created to live.

Aware

When Truman initially became aware something was wrong in his world, he felt confused. His whole life had been immersed in the fake set of a TV show. Writers, directors, producers, and advertisers all had one goal: to keep Truman playing along. But his dissatisfaction with the direction of his life wasn't placated by the new twists they wrote into the script. He flipped from a life of blissful ignorance to a determined search for the truth at any cost. Awareness was the first step on a long journey to discover the life he was really made to live.

After reading this chapter, hopefully you're more aware of something you've probably sensed for a while. Screens are influencing every area of your life, often with damaging results. Even though immersion in technology is the new normal, you may be starting to wonder what can or should be done in response.

In the next two chapters, I'm going to show you something you might not expect: how our constant immersion in technology is able to create desires, influencing everything from what we want for breakfast to who we want for president. I'll follow with a chapter that reveals the plans and motives of those who are in the driver's seat of this cultural transformation. By shaping what we desire, they are able to make us behave as they intend: for their profit, but at our expense.

Many people are unintentionally pulled off-track by the power of screens, unaware of the reason why they are dissatisfied with their life, yet still entangled by the enticing "web." They lament when they compare where they are to where they hoped to be. Unfortunately, their lack of awareness doesn't protect them from the negative consequences of their choices.

But you're no longer unaware.

CHAPTER 2

[UN]PREPARED

HOW YOUR DESIRES ARE SHAPED BY SCREENS

Mind Tricks

"You wanna buy some death sticks?"

Annoyed, the Jedi at the bar discreetly waves his hand and retorts to the young, antennae-clad dealer. "You don't want to sell me death sticks."

Powerless against the Force, the appropriately named Elan Sleazebaggano finds himself strangely compelled to agree, "I don't wanna sell you death sticks."

Obi-Wan sends him away with the now-familiar gesture, injecting the thought into his weak mind. "You want to go home and rethink your life."

With immediate obedience, the now-former death stick pusher turns to leave. "I wanna go home and rethink my life."

What if our desires are being shaped as easily as Mr. Sleazebaggano's? With Jedi-like hand gestures across our screens, what we want to do is being directed by a force that compels us to do its will, often without our knowledge. And just as someone manipulated by the Force is unprepared for its powerful influence, so also our naivety about the power of our screens leaves us dangerously vulnerable.

But not *you*, right? *You're* not weak-minded, right?

I used to think I was above deception, too strong-minded, and unaffected by tricks that would draw other people in. Thankfully, following the practices I'll share later, today I walk in more freedom than ever. And yet, like the smell that unavoidably clings to everyone in a smoke-filled room, the pull of today's screen-saturated world is constant, relentless, and effective.

One day while I was researching this book, I found a documentary about marketing to teens. The video seemed to be right on target, so I started watching. As the narrator revealed techniques used to influence teen behavior, the content quickly turned sexual. Of course, elimination of sexual boundaries has been an obvious goal of media, movies, and music videos, and teens are a prime target. The show was relevant, and yet it quickly became too graphic. Now, I've been free from porn for over twelve years, but these images ignited a familiar twinge of temptation. The cognitive dissonance of wanting to help people with this book while being tempted by what I was seeing confused me for a few minutes. Thankfully, like shaking off an enchantment, I realized what was happening and turned it off. While I started with the desire to help this book's readers through good research, the salacious documentary attempted to shape my desire in a different, and altogether negative, direction.

We are all vulnerable to being pulled in by something on a screen. I imagine you can visualize even now what particularly tempts you. Those images may not be sexualized, but they'll still take you somewhere you don't intend. And if your encounters with screens become habitual, you may wake up years down the road wondering where your time—or maybe your life—has gone.

Do What You Want, or What They Want You to Want

I believe in the reality of free will, which is the power of healthy humans to impact their lives by their authentic, purposeful choices. For example, I'm freely choosing to write this book, and you're freely choosing to read it. (Thank you!) I've blogged in defense of free will[21] at some length, so you can go there to read more if you're interested.

But even as a defender of this foundational God-given human characteristic, I see how, in today's world, our ability to make free choices is being downgraded by a forceful disruption of our decision-making powers. Since desire precedes a free choice, manipulating desires is a powerful way to control people's choices.

Our buying and viewing choices are profitable—especially in our consumer-driven economy. To grow their profits, media leaders want us to spend more time watching and clicking and buying and dressing and eating and drinking and advocating what they choose for us. And what's the best way to make us choose what they want us to choose? By influencing us to *want* to make those choices.

Since so much of screen messaging is focused on influencing our emotions, even the question "What do you want?" has come to mean, "How do you *feel*?" Other aspects of healthy desires, like wisdom, morality, or long-term impact, are pushed to the distant background. This is also intentional, since influencing people emotionally through screens is much easier to do than attempting to guide them rationally through any other means.

"If it feels good, do it!" permeates nearly every message we hear. We know this is not always a good idea. We've seen people do what felt good to them, and now they are addicted, broken, or stuck. Those photos of people devastated by meth shout the contrary message: what feels good sometimes isn't. And yet the message of doing what feels good still sways us.

Here's the masterful and insidious one-two punch. With the left, we're hit with messages like "follow your heart," "go with your gut," "just do it," and, "do what you feel." Then with the right, billions of dollars and millions of hours of content fills our hearts, our guts, and our feelings. What a great system for those who would influence us! They start with the lie that our desires—our feelings—are the truest part of who we are, our very identity. Then, they deploy a global infrastructure to create the desires they want us to have. *They have us in a double-bind: they tell us we should act on our desires, then shape our desires to make us want what they want us to want.*

Want to rethink your life yet?

But there is good news: knowledge is like a vaccine against the double-bind. By learning about the strategies used to shape desire, you'll put yourself on a path to having free, healthy desires aimed at the life you've actually hoped to live.

So, how exactly are our desires shaped? How are we influenced to want what the product producers and online marketers want us to want?

A detailed review of the ways we are influenced by screens would fill many books. But to save you time, I'm packing this chapter with a dense overview of desire-shaping strategies from five points of view: how screens make our brains feel good, how our personal data is used to influence us, how habits are formed, and how some especially "evil" strategies shape our desires. Finally, I'll briefly share how these techniques have been employed for decades through our bigger screens.

How Brains Feel Good

In a December 2016 viral video, Simon Sinek showed how technology becomes addictive—we like the way screens make us feel. He said, "Engagement with social media and our cell phones releases a chemical [in your brain] called dopamine. That's why when you get a text, it feels good. Dopamine is the same chemical that makes us feel good when we smoke, drink, or when we gamble. In other words, it's highly, highly addictive."[22] Seth Godin agrees, linking our connection to our devices with the bell Ivan Pavlov rang to make his dogs salivate.[23] After describing the "hope rush" of dopamine people get when they think about, decide to, and then actually buy a lottery ticket, Godin says,

> The same thing is true for the billion people carrying around a Pavlovian box in their pocket. The smart phone (so called in honor of the profit-seeking companies who were smart enough to make them) is an optimized, tested and polished call-and-response machine. So far, Apple's made a trillion dollars by ringing our bell.[24]

In his important new book, *Irresistible: The Rise of Addictive Technology and the Business of Keeping Us Hooked,* Adam Alter shows how technology activates the same dopamine processes that keep substance addicts addicted.

The human brain exhibits different patterns of activity for different experiences. [. . .] There's also a pattern that describes the brain of a drug addict as he injects heroin, and a second that describes the brain of a gaming addict as he fires up a new World of Warcraft quest. They turn out to be almost identical.

But more recent research has shown that addictive behaviors produce the same brain responses that follow drug abuse. In both cases, several regions deep inside the brain release a chemical called dopamine, which attaches itself to receptors throughout the brain that in turn produce an intense flush of pleasure.[25]

So, both the heroin addict and the WoW addict show the same addictive patterns in their brains, because the dopamine pleasure cycles created by the drug and the video game are identical. This correlation shocked me. Alter continues,

As the brain develops a tolerance, its dopamine-producing regions go into retreat, and the lows between each high dip lower. Instead of producing the healthy measure of dopamine that once inspired optimism and contentment in response to small pleasures, these regions lie dormant until they're overstimulated again. Addictions are so pleasurable that the brain does two things: first it produces less dopamine to dam the flood of euphoria, and then, when the source of that euphoria vanishes, it struggles to cope with the fact it's now producing far less dopamine than it used to. And so the cycle continues as the addict seeks out the source of his addiction, and the brain responds by producing less and less dopamine after each hit.[26]

The same vicious cycle that causes drug addicts to crave more of their drug in order to feel the same pleasure drives screen addicts, and for the same reason. The same amount of screen time, or the same level of game interaction or app usage doesn't make the user feel as good as before, so they must increase their usage to compensate for the decrease in sensitivity caused by their widely fluctuating dopamine imbalance.

The important thing to understand from these experts is that there is a physiological reason we feel good using certain technologies, and the mechanism in the brain is the same as that found in substance abusers. For app designers who want to shape our desires, making us feel good is a sure-fire way to take us where they want us to go.

Alter also cites a study that made a distinction between preference and desire; in other words, liking vs. wanting. There is a difference. Many drug addicts despise their drug for killing them, while they still crave the deadly substance all the more. "What makes addiction so difficult to treat is that wanting is much harder to defeat than liking."[27] I know when I was in the throes of my addiction, I felt the conflict between the guilt, pain, and suffering that it was causing me and my family, and the desire to keep doing it. Alter agrees. "Even as you come to loathe Facebook or Instagram for consuming too much of your time, you continue to want updates as much as you did when they still made you happy."[28]

Here's the bottom line. Our screen-saturated world is able to shape our desires by making us feel good in the same way drugs and alcohol make us feel good, and with similarly undesirable long-term consequences. But how exactly do our screens exploit these brain processes?

More Data Feels Better

Most people don't realize how much data moves between their devices and the giant server farms managed by today's tech and media giants. While your Facebook or Twitter feed appears smooth and predictable to you, behind the scenes there is a torrent of network traffic both coming to you and going out from you. Though you may remember the old days of the internet when you'd click a link to view one web site that replied with one page in response, today, everything you do creates an ongoing conversation between your device and "the cloud." (Did you think your high-speed internet connection was designed for your benefit?)

Further, when I say everything you do is tracked, I mean *everything*. Every swipe and click, for sure, but also every video you watch and how far you watched it; every time you linger over an animated gif or just swipe on by; and certainly everything you ever post, upload, or share is cataloged and linked to the vast amount of data held about you. Over time, the history of every like, pin, email, swipe, and hashtag creates your epic digital biography—literally the instruction book that anyone or anything can read to learn what works on you, and what doesn't.

All of this data feeds advanced machine learning algorithms that help the creators achieve their goals. When a sponsored post appears, your engagement or lack thereof is remembered for the next time, when they'll try a different message, photo, timing, or all of the above. All of your past history is leveraged towards presenting the next content you'll probably like—whatever will keep you scrolling for just a little longer.

It's actually possible to do repeated testing, invisible to you, of nearly every aspect of an app to see what leads to the creator's desired outcome most efficiently. Do you click a red button or a blue button more often? Does the word "like" or just a heart work better? Does this photo work better for men than women, or for millennials better than boomers? Do people with this search history more often click here than there? (You won't believe what happened next!)

Alter summarizes all of this activity well. "The people who create and refine tech, games, and interactive experiences are very good at what they do. They run thousands of tests with millions of users to learn which tweaks work and which ones don't—which background colors, fonts, and audio tones maximize engagement and minimize frustration. *As an experience evolves, it becomes an irresistible, weaponized version of the experience it once was.*"[29]

Intentionally Habit Forming

Our technology doesn't form desires or create addictions by accident. Remember, web sites and apps are some of the most intentionally designed and masterfully deployed creations ever made by humankind (broken links notwithstanding). The builders of these applications have studied the latest psychological, behavioral, and neurological science to ensure we feel the desires they want to create in us.

Nir Eyal, author of *Hooked: How to Build Habit-Forming Products*, details how app developers "manufacture desire." Companies aren't satisfied with just having millions of users, but they must make their apps habit forming in order to really profit from them. The Holy Grail for companies is to create "internal triggers," where we are self-motivated to use their apps on cue without any action on their part. Eyal says,

> A cemented habit is when users subconsciously think, "I'm bored," and instantly Facebook comes to mind. They think, "I wonder what's going on in the world?" and before rational thought occurs, Twitter is the answer. The first-to-mind solution wins.[30]

Eyal describes a four-stage "desire engine" to show how people are led through a predictable process to become habitual users. The engine has four parts: the trigger, action, a variable reward, and commitment.

The *trigger* is the "spark plug" of the engine. A user's relationship with the app or site starts with an external trigger, like an email, a web site link, or a photo in your social feed. The trigger invites the user to take a certain *action*, like clicking the photo. Designers do all they can to encourage the user to take the desired action, especially by making the action simple and by providing *bait*, or a strong motivation.

The *variable reward* is what distinguishes a habit-forming desire engine from a "plain vanilla feedback loop," and is the key of the engine's power to create long-term desires. Predictable feedback loops don't form habits, like when we turn on our faucet and water always comes out. But if, occasionally, wine came out of our faucet, we'd be inclined to turn it off and on repeatedly to see what might happen next. App developers know this, and they add many variable rewards to keep us hooked. Even the anticipation of a possible reward causes a user's dopamine levels to spike before they even open their favorite app.

The last part of the desire engine asks the user to make a *commitment*, and given the pleasure felt from the previous reward, they're ready to commit. Online, commitments include things like giving more time, attention, data, or money. Eyal says well-designed commitments "improve the service for the next go-around," increasing the likelihood the user will engage the next time they are triggered. So, adding more personal information to our LinkedIn profile helps people find us, making it more likely we'll want to check LinkedIn more often and share more data.

The goal of these desire-forming engines is to keep the user cycling through each of these stages repeatedly until they trigger themselves, forging a habit. And, as you know, it works very well. Hundreds of millions of people are self-triggering users, cued by their manipulated desires. So we check our app, take an action, feel the reward, and make more commitments over and over again, unintentionally surrendering our free will in the process.

Forming Habits with Casino Strategies

Developers find inspiration for making screens more habit-forming in many places, including casinos. Delaney Ruston, producer of the excellent *Screenagers*[31] documentary, recently shared how "near misses and short-term rewards that lead to promises of a bigger win are some of the tricks app and game developers have taken from electronic slot machine designers to keep players playing."[32] For example, when slot machines show winning symbols close to the "payline," gamblers feel like they are close to a win, and are inspired to keep playing. Of course, the winning feeling was created by an algorithm that deceived them into thinking they were making progress. Casinos are happy to give away small wins in order to keep the player going long enough to lose even more. The house always wins.

Game developers leverage similar algorithms to keep users engaged longer. Small rewards within a larger quest feed users' desire to make progress. By timing these rewards carefully, in-game purchases can be made more attractive, just like "almost" getting three sevens makes a gambler want to put more money into the slot machine.

Evil by Design

Chris Nodder's disturbingly forthright book, *Evil by Design*, groups powerful desire-shaping software strategies under the famed Seven

Deadly Sins: Pride, Sloth, Gluttony, Anger, Envy, Lust, and Greed. Essentially, by capitalizing on human weaknesses and tendencies to fall for one or more of the Sins, designers can make us do what they want us to do. Nodder's goal is like Eyal's, to teach the industry how to exploit human psychology, with a wink and a nod about whether these exploits should be used for "good" or "evil."

Nodder confirms my thesis in this statement: "Evil design must be intentional."[33] Designers are intentionally creating experiences with "evil" designs to manipulate us, and our lack of preparation leaves us vulnerable. He says, "Sites capitalize on our weaknesses. Sometimes their intentions are good, but mainly they do this for 'evil'—in other words to profit at our expense. The best sites manage to make us feel good at the same time."[34]

Nodder summarizes the desire-manipulation techniques under each of the Seven Sins:

Pride. Use social proof to position your product in line with your visitors' values.

Sloth. Build a path of least resistance that leads users where you want them to go.

Gluttony. Escalate customers' commitment and use loss aversion to keep them there.

Anger. Understand the power of metaphysical arguments and anonymity.

Envy. Create a culture of status around your product and feed aspirational desires.

Lust. Turn desire into commitment by using emotion to defeat rational behavior.

Greed. Keep customers engaged by reinforcing the behaviors you desire.[35]

Nodder's website, http://evildesign.com, shares the 57 designs from his book, all eye-opening and helpful if you want to dig deeper and become more aware of the strategies being "weaponized" and aimed at your weaknesses. I'll share two relevant examples—but keep in mind, there are hundreds of these techniques, all created to make you want to do what they want you to do.

Impatience Leads to Compliance

Interestingly, Nodder grouped *impatience* under the sin of Gluttony, since the impatient consumer typically makes quick decisions in their general hunger for more. Impatient users also more readily agree to terms they might decline if they gave themselves more time to think. Designers can increase impatience by creating a sense of urgency with a time limit. Nodder says people will be more likely to accept potentially more expensive defaults when pressed for time.[36]

A "conversion improvement tool" called Scarcity Builder incites impatience-driven decisions by making it easy to add a countdown timer to any WordPress site. Unprepared consumers who see the seconds ticking by are more likely to take the intended action even if they don't have the money budgeted for whatever is offered. Of course, a digital product can never truly be scarce—but the perception of scarcity still works.

Path of Least Resistance

Under the sin of Sloth, Nodder highlights our tendency to take the *path of least resistance.* He encourages designers to "ensure that your desired end result is on the easiest path through the process. Hide disclaimers in locations away from this path."[37] While it's generally good to make software easy to use, some designs are intentionally exploitative, making the designer's profitable goal *too* easy and potentially addictive.

Streaming video giants like Netflix, Amazon, and YouTube are masters of this strategy. They've created a new cultural addiction we even celebrate: *binge watching,* powered by the quintessential path-of-least-resistance feature, autoplay. Their masterful algorithms accurately predict what you'll be most likely to watch next, since they know everything else you've ever watched, and they know what people like you have watched next. Their goal is to keep you watching as long as possible, and it works.

And why does autoplay work so well? It works because it is simple—we don't have to do anything to accept their goal for us. No decision fatigue, no questioning, no looking for a button to click or a command to type, no asking, "honey, what do you want to watch?" The app just decides what you should watch next. And next, and next, and next. And soon, we're bingeing.

As we saw in the previous chapter, the only competition for binge watching is sleep. Who knows, maybe they'll come up with a computer interface that not only autoplays billions of videos, but keeps us awake through some kind of intravenous feeding. Combined with a Universal Basic Income where we don't have to work, and the video streamers have the perfect formula for 24x7 engagement.

Hyperbole, yes, but are we not on that road? Who would have thought we'd be where we are now, spending an average of twelve hours every day consuming media? And we're consuming this media because desire-shaping strategies like these work on unintentional people.

It's Not Just the Apps

Software isn't the only tool used to ensnare us. Pervasive video content is shaping our desires like never before. Of course, TV shows and commercials have been pastoring culture for decades, but even so, most of us are unprepared for the way they shape our entire view of reality, build our expectations of how the world should operate, and influence how we live our lives.

In the prophetic and never-more-relevant book *Amusing Ourselves To Death*, Dr. Neil Postman warned of the consequences of a TV-driven culture. Today, as many consider *Game of Thrones* a sign of a "new golden age of television,"[38] few recognize the power of the video we consume to change the way we think. Postman's message is a desperately needed wake-up call.

Postman argued that TV destroys our ability to make rational decisions. While we like to think we are careful decision-makers, our immersion in screens has essentially rendered our rationality impotent. Postman says, "to be rationally considered, any claim—commercial or otherwise—must be made in language."[39] In other words, we can't even think about something as being true or false until it is expressed as a proposition—a claim about reality. For example, if I were to show you nutritional data of a Big Mac and compared it to homemade lentil soup, I could convince you that, indeed, the soup is much better for you. Then why do so many people opt for the cheeseburger? Could it be that the billions of dollars spent on millions of hours of commercials showing beautiful, smiling people loving their lives while they eat at McDonald's actually works?

Advertisers like McDonald's know if they make us feel like our lives will be happier, if they make it easy for us to go there, and if they architect the food with intentionally addictive recipes,[40] we'll disregard our rational desire to be healthy and go with how we feel. Our desires have been manipulated to take us to an unhealthy destination. Studies show even the presence of healthy items on the menu is enough to make a person think they've made a healthy choice, so they'll be okay with going for the unhealthy option.

As Postman says, "One can like or dislike a television commercial, of course. But one cannot refute it."[41] He masterfully shows how commercials aren't about promoting the benefits of products to help us make a rational choice. Instead, they are about telling us a story about ourselves, making us *feel* like we are the kind of people who buy what they're selling. "The television commercial is not at all about the character of products to be consumed. It is about the character of the consumers of products."[42]

At the movie theater recently, my wife and I saw a commercial for a new SUV. The ad was a perfect example of what Postman calls a "psycho-drama," a story designed to make us associate positive, heartfelt feelings with this car and its maker. In the story, a man, a woman, two kids, and a grandmother are on a cross-country car trip. We see them laughing, hugging, and awestruck in the presence of beautiful landmarks. They end up at a diner frequented by the grandmother and her recently deceased husband. Grandma breaks down in tears, lamenting that her love was not able to join them, while the grandkids comfort her. After seeing this commercial, my wife leaned over and said she wanted this car—and we've been talking about my research for years! She *knew* she wanted the car because she fell in love with the grandmother in less than sixty seconds. Like my wife, everyone watching wished the grandmother's husband was alive to enjoy their trip. After one minute, we felt real feelings for these actors and their fictional life. Their fake tears evoked real ones in us. And *that* is how desires are shaped.

Postman called commercials "parables," choosing the term as a direct link to biblical parables. He says, "The television commercial is about products only in the sense that the story of Jonah is about the anatomy of whales, which is to say, it isn't. Which is to say further, it is about how one ought to live one's life."[43] The millions of commercials, TV shows, and movies we see teach us how we should see the world, and assign to us the role they want us to play. They are parables about what a good life is, and especially how (and how quickly) problems should be solved. And all the time, money, and effort invested into them works.

Where does all of the desire-shaping power lead? I, like Postman, think the stakes are higher than any of us imagine. It's just not just that we'll waste money or time. It's not even just about our own life being filled with regrettable decisions. Here's Postman's summary and prophetic warning:

> "What Huxley teaches [in his book *Brave New World*] is that in the age of advanced technology, spiritual devastation is more likely to come from an enemy with a smiling face than from one whose countenance exudes suspicion and hate. In the Huxleyan prophecy, Big Brother does not watch us, by his choice. We watch him, by ours. There is no need for wardens or gates or Ministries of Truth. When a population becomes distracted by trivia, when cultural life is redefined as a perpetual round of entertainments, when serious public conversations become a form of baby-talk, when, in short, a people become an audience and their public business a vaudeville act, then a nation finds itself at risk; *culture-death is a clear possibility.*"[44]

Prepared

In this chapter, I've exposed you to several of the powerful, *weaponized*, desire-forming methods aimed at each of us. First, we saw how the message of "doing what feels good" is combined with deliberate techniques that manipulate the brain's pleasure mechanisms. Just as the cat comes running when she hears the can opener pierce through a tuna can, so also we are drawn to the "pop" of carefully crafted messages, images, sounds, or app designs.

Through Nir Eyal's *desire engine*, we learned how habits are formed by designs that intentionally manipulate our pleasure centers and psychological makeup. Starting with an external trigger, we take an action, hoping for a reward designed to encourage new levels of commitment. If we go around enough times, we'll habitually volunteer for new trips through the cycle with our phones and remote controls. Chris Nodder followed, teaching us many of the Evil Designs aimed at exploiting human weaknesses to tempt us to go where designers want to take us.

Finally, Neil Postman showed how entertainment has become a framework for interpreting reality itself. Since we are so accustomed to the rhythm of TV commercials, shows, and their digital counterparts, we come to see the real world as just another episode. And all of this reinforces a goal of leading us through our feelings, and away from reasonable, thoughtful decision making.

Time is the magic ingredient that makes every strategy effective. The most alluring media is ineffective unless we spend time with it. But with constant proximity to screens, our desires are orchestrated like a symphony. Because we've spent hours "practicing," we're ready to play our part, right on cue.

And drawing us in to spend more time is the goal. Keep watching, play just a little longer, and binge away. The more we play and watch and swipe, the more we'll want to, and those who've spent countless hours determining how best to manipulate our decision making process will have a customer for life. By playing along, we freely give away our most precious asset: our time and attention. As David Heinemeier Hansen (DHH) says, "The defense [of app companies] is that this is how we get these apps for free. How oxymoronic. Here's this thing for "free," if you give me the most valuable things you own: your attention, your privacy, your peace of mind. The price tag may say $0, but it ain't free."[45]

The creators know a secret we often forget: we only really care about what we see. How could it be otherwise? We can only care about what we're aware of, and awareness comes from our senses. The couple five houses down might be going through a divorce, the elderly shut-in might be feeling worthless, or that teenager in the bedroom down the hall might be desperate, but we don't care if we don't see any of this actually happening. When we spend so much time engaged with our screens and focused on what the creators want us to care about, our real lives, real people, and real needs around us can be sorely neglected.

In the wake of all that is intentionally aimed at us, what should we do? How can we rise above the media influence and ground our desires, our decisions and our lives on what is really good and right and true? How can we break free and allow our desires to be shaped by God himself?

The practices I'll share in later chapters will answer these questions and more. But first, it's important to understand not only how our desires are shaped, but by whom, and for what purpose. By learning the motives of those who are leveraging all of this desire-manipulating power, I think you'll feel a more urgent need to flip the intentionality imbalance. My goal is to help you understand so that you'll become more intentional over the direction of your life than they are—for good.

Even before we get there, I hope you'll never look at another screen without considering what the creator of the content you're watching wants you to desire—that is, what real-life Jedi mind tricks might be at work. Ask yourself: Why do I *really* want to (do / see / hear / buy / wear / eat / drink / post) this, and *who am I becoming as a result*?

If you keep this question in mind, you'll be *prepared* for the next screen you see.

CHAPTER 3

[UN]PRINCIPLED

WHO IS INTENTIONALLY SHAPING YOUR DESIRES, AND WHY

Unintended Consequences?

"*What have we done?*" Breathless and trembling, Bilbo gripped the rocks outside the cave as the enormous winged beast rocketed from the core of the Lonely Mountain.

As the hobbit anticipated the fiery devastation Smaug the Destroyer would discharge upon the vulnerable Lake-town, he regretted his role in the quest to oust the dragon. In Tolkien's tale, Thorin Oakenshield and his fellow dwarves were eager to retake their mountain kingdom, completely focused on their pursuit of the treasure and its power. But now that the dragon was awakened and about to burn hundreds of villagers, Bilbo saw the terrible side effects of their treasure hunt—and it wasn't worth the loss of precious lives.

Among the mountains surrounding Silicon Valley, thousands of developers have labored for years to build the amazing technologies that surround us. The adrenaline, caffeine, pizza, and beer-fueled efforts are often motivated by the promise of giant rewards if they go *viral*—the magic word, shiny as the gold sought by California miners from another century. Those "unicorns" who would find their pot of gold at the end of the rainbow often make world-changing promises to venture capitalists, hoping they'll be funded long enough for a Google or a Facebook to take notice from on high and acquire them.

And yet, after years of breathless innovation, some who were twenty-somethings willing to be buried in code for 80 hours a week have grown up into thirty-somethings with families. Now with kids of their own, some of them are starting to question the cost of the intentionally habit-forming strategies they've embedded into their products to make them go *viral*.

One such questioner is Tony Fadell, a former senior vice president at Apple and inventor of the Nest smart thermostat. Though he was a major influence on the development of the iPod and the iPhone, he has been expressing some regrets. Here's what Fadell told a London Design Museum audience:

> I wake up in cold sweats every so often thinking, what did we bring to the world? Did we really bring a nuclear bomb with information that can–like we see with fake news–blow up people's brains and reprogram them? Or did we bring light to people who never had information, who can now be empowered?[46]

Fadell realizes the technology-obsessed world he helped to create is "one in which screens are everywhere, distracting us and interrupting what's important, while promoting a culture of self-aggrandizement. He says that addiction has been designed into our devices—and it's harming the newest generation."[47]

While Fadell believes most of the designers of our devices didn't mean to hurt anyone, the impact is the same. As we've seen in previous chapters, their intentionally desire-shaping strategies are working very well, amassing mountains of gold for the creators while leaving many users distracted or addicted.

Even if the brilliant designers and developers who crafted our immersive technologies didn't see the potential for bad side effects, it seems that their leaders were not so ignorant. As Adam Alter shows in his prologue to *Irresistible*, Steve Jobs refused to let his kids use the iPad.[48] Alter cites a 2010 *New York Times* article where Jobs is quoted as saying, "We limit how much technology our kids use in the home."

Alter continues, listing several other technology leaders who kept devices from their kids:

> Evan Williams, a founder of Blogger, Twitter, and Medium, bought hundreds of books for his two young sons, but refused to give them an iPad. And Lesley Gold, the founder of an analytics company, imposed a strict no-screen-time-during-the-week rule on her kids. [...] It seemed as if the people producing tech products were following the cardinal rule of drug dealing: never get high on your own supply.[49]

These leaders know the risks of their products enough to protect their own kids, yet they keep using intentionally desire-shaping techniques to build the fastest growing empires the world has ever seen.

Climbing the Lonely Mountain

It's hard to notice how much things are changing while we're living through the changes. Kids grow up before our eyes, but without those old photos, the differences over time aren't clear. But indeed, the beautiful young woman in her wedding gown really was a little girl in a Cinderella costume not long ago.

Technological changes are like that. Over time, we recognize that our world has been transformed. Individually, we only see our personal, gradual changes: the flatter screens, faster phones, and higher-speed connections. We hardly notice that billions of us on the same journey have transformed the world economy by becoming—often unintentionally—compulsive users.

The five most valuable publicly-traded companies in the U.S. stock market back in 2001 were familiar names from diverse industries: General Electric, Microsoft, Exxon, Citigroup, and Walmart. From that list, only one was a technology company; the others, a cross-section of manufacturing, energy, finance, and retail. Fast-forward to 2017, when the top five were today's household (and handheld) names: Apple, Google (as Alphabet, Inc.), Microsoft, Amazon, and Facebook.[50] That's a huge change in 16 years. Our economy is now dominated by the companies who fill our eyes and minds.

Scott Galloway, an entrepreneur, investor, and self-described "Professor of Marketing" as a faculty member at NYU's Stern School of Business, recently published *The Four: The Hidden DNA of Amazon, Apple, Facebook, and Google.* He likens the "Four" to the Biblical Four Horsemen of the Apocalypse, though he also celebrates them as the Four Horsemen of "god, love, sex, and consumption."[51] Galloway's style is irreverent (and sometimes profane), but his analysis is enlightening.

Apple, "the most profitable company in history,"[52] makes 74% of its revenue from iPhone & iPad sales, with another 10% selling Macs. Amazon earns almost 90% of its income by selling products, streaming video and music, and by dominating retail, and is currently valued higher than Walmart, Target, Macy's, Kroger, Ikea, and five other huge retailers, *combined.*[53] Nearly 90% of Google's earnings come from advertising via Search and YouTube, leading them to eclipse the combined value of the eight next largest media companies *combined,* including Disney, Comcast, and Time Warner.[54] Facebook is even more dependent on advertising with 97% of their billions coming from ads shared with their more than two billion users.[55]

It's striking how dominant these companies have become by either selling our attention (ads), or the means for capturing our attention (devices). They seem to find our time and attention more valuable than we do, since we are often so unintentional with both. Their intentionally desire-shaping strategies have been leading us to make decisions worth mountains of cash—complete with dragon-like power and influence.

And the Four horsemen have a symbiotic relationship with each other as they dominate our lives. While competing fiercely with each other, they are also powerful allies. Facebook properties open the "top of the funnel" for the others, as we see friends, celebrities, and ads for products and adventures we're enticed to desire. We then search Google to find those things, and Amazon, as Google's largest advertiser,[56] is most often at the top of the list. We do all of this on our Apple devices, which must be continually upgraded with higher speed and visual capabilities so we can more quickly see our latest "needs" in the highest possible resolution.

Conquer at Any Cost

In one sense, to see companies winning at this level is inspiring. We admire hard work and determination and like to see former underdogs like Apple win by making superior products over time. College-dropout-to-billionaire stories like Facebook founder Mark Zuckerberg's are what many kids aspire to achieve. Who can fault them? Free markets and capitalism for the win, right?

Winning is only valid if one "competes according to the rules" (2 Timothy 2:5). We don't admire cheaters. When we learned how professional baseball players were taking steroids so they could beat long-held home run records, we lost respect for them. In a way, they were trying to change the rules of the game. In their ambition to win at any cost, they tried to gain super-human strength to do what players before were physically unable to achieve.

It's the same with the Four, and other companies like them. Once they're big enough to become a publicly traded company, the financial markets demand one thing: growth, regardless of what unprincipled rule-bending may be necessary. With enough money, companies get to remake the rules, and often avoid the unfortunate side-effects of their conquest.

David Heinemeier Hansson (DHH),[57] an influential tech industry leader, wrote an insightful and blistering critique of the industry in a 2017 *Medium* article. He says, "There is no higher God in Silicon Valley than growth. No sacrifice too big for its craving altar. As long as you keep your curve exponential, all your sins will be forgotten at the exit."[58] Market pressures don't just motivate companies to build great products, but to continually grow the *potential* of a world-dominating product. How is that achieved? Through a process that rewards those who attract the most users, using the intentionally addictive strategies we saw in chapter 2. DHH says it this way: "It's a hyper-evolutionary process that rewards the most extractive, most addictive, most viral strain from the cohort. The key measurement is ENGAGEMENT. Who cares about the virtue of the endeavor, as long as your product is maximally addictive?"[59] The system itself rewards those who turn the most enthusiastic users into addicts.

Facebook and Google (especially through YouTube) know how to harvest our attention better than anyone else. They have conquered their markets by freely sharing their services with anyone willing to give their time, attention, and privacy in return. Here's their little secret: anytime you use a "free" app or service, *you are the product.* If you're not a paying customer, someone else is. For Facebook and Google (and all the smaller companies that mimic them), their customers aren't you and me; their customers are their advertisers. Their advanced data-mining platforms squeeze every drop of information out of the attention we freely give them. In return, we get perfectly targeted, desire-forming content and ads. The advertisers get what they pay for: *us,* served on a silver-screened platter.

Combine their endless store of personal information with their addictive strategies to entice us to spend more time on their platforms, and you have a recipe for unprincipled conquest.

These companies have conquered each of their markets: Amazon in retail, Facebook in social media, Google in all other media, and Apple in . . . being Apple. If these companies are "eating the world"[60] by manipulating us and exploiting their power to destroy competition, why are most of us so willing, even enthusiastic, to go along with them?

Ultimately, they make us happy to be conquered. Through the masterful use of marketing, positioning, and public relations strategies pioneered nearly a hundred years ago, they shape our desires. Back then, they called it what it was: *propaganda.*

Propaganda, the Key to Conquest

Edward Bernays (1891-1995) may be the most influential person of the twentieth century you've never heard of. The nephew of Sigmund Freud is considered the "father of public relations."[61] By combining what he learned from reading his uncle Sigmund's theories on psychoanalysis with new learnings on crowd psychology, he pioneered methods to influence the public that have never been more powerful.

One of his most notorious "public relations" achievements was to influence women in the late 1920s to buy more cigarettes from his client, American Tobacco Company. In those days, a woman smoking in public was a major social taboo.

To overcome the public's negative view of women smoking, Bernays staged a spectacle at the 1929 Easter Parade in New York City. He hired fashion models to walk in the parade and at a coordinated moment, light up their now rebranded "torches of freedom."[62] Bernays informed major news outlets so they would be ready to cover and photograph the demonstration, using one of his favorite techniques: free promotion as "news" coverage. Unfortunately, the plan worked well. What a devious manipulation—convince people to see an addictive and enslaving product as a path to "freedom."

Might our screens be the same to us today?

None of us want to believe we live in a world where a few elites are manipulating the rest of us for their profit, and to our detriment. We are led to scoff at "conspiracy theories," and certainly, we should be skeptical. But when the effectiveness of the manipulator is so public, and he is so brazen in his self-promotion, the "conspiracy" perpetrated on us is too obvious to ignore. Listen to Bernays's own words:

> The conscious and intelligent manipulation of the organized habits and opinions of the masses is an important element in democratic society. Those who manipulate this unseen mechanism of society constitute an invisible government which is the true ruling power of our country. We are governed, our minds molded, our tastes formed, our ideas suggested, largely by men we have never heard of.[63]

The boldness and clarity with which Bernays makes this statement is chilling. He declares that we are under the power of an "invisible government," and that our desires are shaped by them. Not only are they doing this, but he claims "intelligent manipulation" is *necessary* in a democracy like ours. Manipulation and democracy don't seem like they should go together.

But Bernays presents this situation as a "fact," regardless of what the rest of us think about being manipulated.

Whatever attitude one chooses toward this condition, it remains a fact that in almost every act of our daily lives, whether in the sphere of politics or business, in our social conduct or our ethical thinking, we are dominated by the relatively small number of persons—a trifling fraction of our hundred and twenty million—who understand the mental processes and social patterns of the masses. It is they who pull the wires which control the public mind, who harness old social forces and contrive new ways to bind and guide the world.[64]

Note the elitist thinking, the implied superiority, and how he thinks that there are just a "trifling fraction" of the population who can comprehend how the rest of us should think and act. This may be what is happening in practice—not because of our inability, but because of our ignorance of the process. We are blind and vulnerable to these things not because we are inferior, but because we are unaware.

Some of the phenomena of this process are criticized— the manipulation of news, the inflation of personality, and the general ballyhoo by which politicians and commercial products and social ideas are brought to the consciousness of the masses. The instruments by which public opinion is organized and focused may be misused. But such organization and focusing are necessary to orderly life.

As civilization has become more complex, and as the need for invisible government has been increasingly demonstrated, the technical means have been invented and developed by which opinion may be regimented.[65]

Re-read that last sentence. Certainly, technical means to manipulate the public were available in the 1920s, like newspapers, magazines, and radio. But those pale in comparison to today's technologies, which "regiment" our opinions, desires, and ultimately our decisions in ways that would make Bernays salivate.

I find Bernays's use of the word "regimented" most telling. He's saying that the goal of the "invisible government" is to cause our thinking to fall in line like a military brigade—each of us marching to the orders of our trusted, unseen leaders. Through repetition of messages that promote whatever we are to be enticed to desire or reject, our thinking is brought in line, like an army regiment, ready to follow another's orders to want, buy, watch, click, swipe, or even vote on command.

How insidious! Because our desires themselves are being manipulated, we actually *want* to do what we are being *regimented* to do. We want to act like the celebrities on TV, to listen to music that devalues women and minorities, to watch movies that celebrate immorality, or to waste our lives playing games or binging on the latest show. We are the ones who ultimately pay for subscriptions, buy the devices, click the clickbait. We're doing all this because we *want* to, and we want to because we've been *regimented* to do so.

In the early 60's, Aldous Huxley, the author Neil Postman cited in the previous chapter, prophesied how desire manipulation would be used to control us in the future:

> There will be, in the next generation or so, a pharmacological method of making people love their servitude, and producing dictatorship without tears, so to speak, producing a kind of painless concentration camp for entire societies, **so that people will in fact have their liberties taken away from them, but will rather enjoy it, because they will be distracted from any desire to rebel by propaganda or brainwashing**, or brainwashing enhanced by pharmacological methods. And this seems to be the final revolution.[66]

The techniques of propaganda pioneered by Bernays are actively used in nearly every sector of our society: food, fashion, cars, houses, education, travel. However, for this book's theme, I'll stick to examples related to technology and screens.

Modern Propaganda

In a recent speech, Mark Zuckerberg laid out a new vision for Facebook—to bring the world closer together through communities. You can read the whole transcript at the footnoted link.[67]

"Zuck" is very relatable; he talks about his daughter, his dog, and his dad. He then speaks about the core human need for community. He lauds people by name who have used Facebook groups to improve their neighborhoods and causes, affecting millions of lives. Those who say Zuck has presidential aspirations (he'll be barely old enough in 2020—so it could happen) might be on to something. His style is on par with other winning candidates.

In this speech, he compares Facebook communities to church and other traditionally in-person communities, claiming near equality between real and online connections. He promotes Facebook as the answer to the decline in people's participation in physical community organizations. Zuck proclaims:

> So now we're setting a goal—to help one billion people join meaningful communities. If we can do this, it will not only turn around the whole decline in community membership we've seen for decades, it will start to strengthen our social fabric and bring the world closer together.[68]

Who doesn't want meaningful community? Who doesn't want to bring the world closer together? Zuck, using Bernaysian techniques from his great-grandfather's generation, links into these legitimate and vital human needs by offering to solve them for us.

But think about it. What happens if one billion people join "meaningful" Facebook communities? Those one billion people will be more engaged than ever—with Facebook! A billion more humans will be even more valuable "products" to sell to advertisers, which will further enable Facebook's cycle of conquest, consuming more of people's time, privacy, and lives.

Remember, Zuckerberg isn't running a charity, yet he speaks like he is. He draws us in with stories of love and community and pets and connection, but his goal—his ultimate goal—is to serve his customer. But remember: *you are not his customer.*

In Zuck's 2017 commencement speech to Harvard, the college he dropped out of to start Facebook, he uses the same relatable storytelling to promote an even more nefarious idea. He makes himself out to be just another entrepreneur, a regular guy who hit the big time a little bigger than others. He endears himself to his audience effectively.

He challenges the graduates to do two things: help "create a world where everyone has a sense of purpose," and, "redefin[e] equality to give everyone the freedom they need to pursue purpose."[69] Of course, everyone seeks purpose, equality, and freedom. But there's something very Bernaysian in his next proposal.

Zuckerberg says, "The greatest successes come from having the freedom to fail," and, "right now our society is way over-indexed on rewarding success and we don't do nearly enough to make it easy for everyone to take lots of shots." After sharing more endearing words that make him sound like just another lucky entrepreneur who is still just like the rest of us, he says:

> We should have a society that measures progress not just by economic metrics like GDP, but by how many of us have a role we find meaningful. We should explore ideas like universal basic income to give everyone a cushion to try new things.[70]

Jeff Bezos, CEO of Amazon, recently promoted the same idea of a universal basic income.[71] Both of these billionaires—while actively destroying whole segments of the economy by their business practices and manipulation of our desires[72]—have supported the growing movement towards a Universal Basic Income (UBI). UBI is a stipend, often proposed to be around $10,000/year, given to every person by the government so their basic needs are met without having to worry about keeping a job. What could possibly go wrong?

Remember, the technological kingdoms of those like Bezos and Zuckerberg have been built by exploiting you and your desires, and by leveraging their huge wealth to displace entire industries. They have conquered just as any other invader of ages ago conquered, by doing everything possible to completely overwhelm their enemy until they are the only ruler in town.

Now empowered and the only leaders left standing, they recognize how the economy they have reshaped for conquest may not work out well for the masses. So, from their ivory towers, awash in their billions (Bezos is currently the richest person in the world,[73] and Zuck is third richest),[74] they propose to share the government's money—your tax dollars—with everyone.

Could it be that our screen immersion has robbed us of our ability to think, learn, and innovate in ways that would have helped us all build a truly robust economy, not one that just benefits the powerful and well-connected? Could it be that while we've all been watching Amazon or Netflix or YouTube or Instagram or Snapchat, we've wasted time we could have spent adapting and growing and shaping the world with opportunity for the many instead of vast treasure troves for the few?

As Galloway ends *The Four*, he explains why people who were angry enough to vote for Trump[75] should have been aiming their wrath at the tech sector more than globalization and immigration: "The tech economy, and its fetishization, is as much to blame. It has dumped an enormous amount of wealth into the laps of a small cohort of investors and incredibly talented workers—leaving much of the workforce behind (perhaps believing the opiate of the masses will be streaming video content and a crazy-powerful phone)."[76] A little later in the book, he says:

> We have a perception of these large companies that they must be creating a lot of jobs, but in fact they have a small number of high-paying jobs, and everybody else is fighting over the scraps. **America is on pace to be home to 3 million lords and 350 million serfs.**[77]

DHH agrees. After lambasting Uber for enriching their leaders on the backs of millions of drivers who make minimum wage while getting the "freedom to choose between working 60 or 80 hours a week to make ends meet," he says:

> If nothing changes, we'll continue to vest the tech titans and their lords with economic monopolies that grant them undue power. They're too big to be conscientious. "Don't be evil" is a slogan for an upstart, not a conglomerate. You simply can't distribute such noble a moral codex across endless divisions, all with their own P&Ls.

And don't fall for the soothing charity by the extractive victors either. That charade is as old as time. It's the process by which ruthless tech lords seek to rebrand themselves into noble benefactors for the good of society. By giving back some of their spoils as they see fit. Kings of plenty doling out gifts and mercy. Don't buy it. And I don't mean that in the sense that, say, Bill Gates hasn't done good with his fortune. **But that society isn't better off when we have to rely on magnanimous tech lords to solve its ills by decree.**[78]

Are you OK being one of the 350 million serfs? Seeing thousands of your neighbors struggling when, in the aftermath of our deformed screen-saturated economy, they've all been anesthetized into self-focused, consumption-minded drones? Who, while receiving their "generous" UBI, become angry when they can't buy what they see on Instagram anymore?

Beyond the Four

Before we close this chapter, I need to share some of the more insidious and destructively unprincipled producers who are intentionally using screens to shape our desires in an even darker direction.

Back on the theme of incremental change, TV has certainly morphed over the decades, and our tastes have been shaped accordingly. In 1967, the most popular TV program was *The Andy Griffith Show*. Ten years later, it was *Laverne & Shirley*. Another ten—*The Golden Girls*. Fast forward to this decade, where *Game of Thrones (GoT)* and *Breaking Bad* top the list.[79] From Andy Griffith to Walter White is not an upgrade. Ask yourself: what TV world would you rather your kids grow up in?

My friends at Covenant Eyes say, "If you're watching *Game of Thrones*, you're watching porn."[80] How did we get from Mayberry to where the most popular show is outright pornography? Most of us unintentionally went along with the changes, while the creators intentionally took us on this journey, shaping our desires and ultimately changing society.

Here's evidence. In a 2012 interview with Neil Marshall, one of *GoT's* directors, he said, "The weirdest part [of directing *Game of Thrones*] was when you have one of the exec producers leaning over your shoulder, going, 'You can go full frontal, you know. This is television, you can do whatever you want! And do it! I urge you to do it!' So I was like, 'Okay, well, you're the boss.'" He went on to say, "This particular exec took me to one side and said, 'Look, I represent the pervert side of the audience, okay? Everybody else is the serious drama side, [but] I represent the perv side of the audience, and I'm saying I want full frontal nudity in this scene.' So you go ahead and do it."[81]

Armed with a producer who wants to represent the "pervert side of the audience," *GoT* "goes ahead and does it," over and over again. *Intentionally.* And today, it's popular, accepted, and discussed in every corner of society—including the church—as normal. But why is the unnamed producer doing this? Because he wants people to watch it, and to *want* to watch it. He's *shaping our desires.* He produces perverted content that ends up creating an audience who wants more of his kind of content. As a result, all of the viewers become "the perv side."

We might be able to thank the recently departed Hugh Hefner for some of our willingness to accept porn in the mainstream. The billionaire founder of Playboy Enterprises was a master of Bernaysian propaganda. He was eulogized as a brave advocate of free speech and general liberty. With the same upside-down logic as calling a cigarette a "torch of freedom," Hefner is quoted as saying: "The major civilizing force in the world is not religion, it is sex."[82]

But Hefner's vision of sex was carefully crafted to move culture directly where we are today. In a brilliant 2003 *Christianity Today* article, Read Mercer Schuchardt correctly identifies Hefner's propaganda:

> As a mythmaker on the scale of Walt Disney, Hugh Hefner did for porn what Henry Higgins did for Eliza Doolittle.[83]
>
> As an adman, Hefner saw the need to package sexuality into aspirational categories, to tell a story about it that placed men in the narrative itself in a way that was not just acceptable but downright desirable. Thus, he packaged himself as a Victorian gentleman at the hunting lodge.

> Credit Hefner with popularizing the mythology that this was "adult" entertainment for "men," adding the same aura of pseudo-sophistication that is still exploited 50 years later by bars that call themselves "A Gentleman's Club."[84]

Hefner succeeded in using propaganda techniques to recast the terms "adult," "free," and "gentleman" to mean their opposite. "Adult" entertainment is really for those who would be childish; the "freedom" is really enslavement and addiction; and no "gentleman" would treat women like Hefner did. But the porn industry and now mainstream television is still reading from Hef's script.

The biggest industry-lobbying group for the "adult entertainment" industry has a sickeningly Bernaysian name—the "Free Speech Coalition (FSC)." Under the blanket of the First Amendment to the U.S. Constitution, which was never intended by any Founder to apply to porn, the FSC has successfully convinced courts all the way to the U.S. Supreme Court to overturn obscenity laws and make porn completely acceptable across the land.

Because porn is so accessible today on every device and our culture has become so pornified, it's almost unthinkable that society ever saw anything as obscene. In a culture that celebrates *Fifty Shades of Gray* as an appropriate Valentine's Day movie, we've completely lost our former moorings. But thanks to effective propaganda from the FSC and a rebranding of "free speech," the courts decreed the legal production of virtually every kind of pornography, even porn that depicts sex with minors,[85] as long as the actors aren't actually minors.

The video game industry has its own propaganda machine, a powerful lobbying group called the Entertainment Software Association (ESA). Nearly 90% of the gaming industry, which earned $30.4 billion in 2016,[86] belong to the ESA. They are also very effective in reshaping the intent of "free speech" in their interests, for their profit, but at our society's expense.

Everyone knows that video games have become more violent over time. The comparison between *Pong* and *Call of Duty* is similar to contrasting Mayberry and Westeros (what a pornified name—West*eros*). Each time there is a school shooting, lawmakers from both sides of the aisle call for investigations into the impact of violent video games. And every time, the ESA is there to help politicians understand why they should "move along... nothing to see here. Remember: 'FREE SPEECH'."

Does "free speech" mean we should want our neighbors to pretend to urinate on someone before burning them alive (seen in *Postal 2*), or we want our daughters to be dating guys who have been pretending to rape and otherwise violate women for hours each day? Is that really what Thomas Jefferson and friends had in mind when they ensured our republic would protect "free speech?"

It takes a lot of money and effort to help everyone forget their common sense and disconnect the obvious link between what you think about, practice, or pretend to do, and what you actually do. But they tirelessly do it—just Google (the source of Truth) for the link between violent video games and physical violence, and you'll find a treasure trove of ESA propaganda.

ESA has spent tens of millions of dollars lobbying legislatures, fighting court battles, and contributing to federal, state, and local campaigns for Republicans and Democrats. Here's one example documented in an excellent and disturbing paper written by Dr. Jennifer M. Proffitt and Dr. Margot A. Susca of Florida State University.[87] In 2005, then Senator Hillary Clinton and Senator Joseph Lieberman proposed the Family Entertainment Protection Act (SB 2126), a federal law to protect minors from explicit games. That year, ESA representatives hosted a $1,000-a-plate fundraiser for Clinton. ESA also spent $120,000 lobbying against this bill. After just one year, Clinton and Lieberman announced a new plan: let the industry continue to regulate itself. The bill died in committee.[88]

There are hundreds of such examples. Each one shows the power of a giant industry to leverage its mountain of cash to create unprincipled rules, allowing them to exploit their audience. The feedback loop is the same as for all addictive screen content—design the games to be addictive, encourage people to play them more, then increase the "edginess"—because, just as with drug addiction, it takes more and more dopamine in the brain to give the same sensation as before. All in the interest of generating enormous profits for the makers at the expense of the lives and futures of the players.

Some gaming advocates really push the propaganda envelope, celebrating the lifestyle of the (now unfortunately stereotypical) young man in his parent's basement playing *World of Warcraft*. In a recent *Breakpoint* podcast, John Stonestreet quoted gamer Peter Suderman.

> These digital opiates provide what he calls "a baseline level of daily happiness, serving as a buffer between the player and despair." As one game designer put it, they fulfill a fantasy of "work, purpose, and social and professional success." Video games, concludes Suderman, "offer a sort of **universal basic income for the soul**."[89]

He's suggesting that gaming replaces real-world work, filling the same part of us as a real purpose would fill. A UBI for the soul? What about Zuckerberg's claim in support of the monetary UBI proposal that people will be free to take risks if they aren't afraid of failing and losing a job? It seems that instead, people will be free to buy and play more video games, which apparently meets the same need.

See the intentional, unprincipled, self-serving cycle here? Create addictive experiences, keep anyone from regulating them, and then, when obsession or violent actions happen, downplay the links. They conquer by building an empire on the backs of those who could otherwise take their creative energy, learn real skills, and make real innovations that would make a positive difference in the world.

Intentionally Unprincipled

We now know that the elites who use screens to shape our desires share the same motivation as Tolkien's dwarves of Erebor—to capture a mountain full of gold. And instead of swords and shields, they use Bernaysian methods to "regiment" our minds, enticing us to stay plugged into their monetizing schemes so we'll willingly increase their hoard. They use their growing power to crush competition and keep governments in line, so nothing stands in the way of their conquest.

This is the part where a lot of authors would give qualifying statements. "It's not all bad. Look at all the good these technologies have brought to us." Or, "we just need balance." These claims have a measure of truth in them, but they let us off the hook too easy. They keep us from having to really consider what is happening. They produce a sort of resignation—making us think things like, "It's just the way it is. Screens aren't going anywhere." Or, "this is the world we live in, so, what can I do?"

I'll tell you what you can do: *you can become more intentional about your own life than they are.* You can let what you've learned upset you—maybe even anger you. You can marvel at the level of power and influence they've amassed by exploiting most of us, making us feel good while we waste our lives. You can be amazed at the hutzpah of a leader like Zuckerberg who can talk about giving people meaning and purpose in lofty speeches while his platforms and strategies replace real-world meaning and purpose with self-focused addictions.

And, you can stay with me as we find biblical practices that, like nothing else, can enable us to walk in true freedom through a world bent on influencing our every thought—from morning until night, cradle to grave. But before we get to those practices, we must consider what the Bible has to say about the current state of the world, how we got here, and what else might be going on behind the scenes. Far from being an old, irrelevant text, the Bible actually anticipated these times. In fact, I believe the only solid answers to today's tech-immersed world come from the Scriptures. I think you'll agree.

For now, remember, there are unprincipled people with powerful platforms who are willing to use every possible tool to shape our desires into profits for them, and loss for us. Without guiding principles that put the highest good of all people—their actual freedom and value—above doing whatever it takes to please shareholders, they can exploit without limit. They make us feel good all the way to a life we regret, because we end up with nothing but the empty things they sold us, and the wasted time we could have used to make a real difference in the world.

We all know we were made for more. There is meaning and purpose to be found, but neither one of these are going to be found in the unintentional use of a screen. Only those who are willing to be more intentional with their lives than the billionaires who want to control us will find the meaning and purpose we long for.

CHAPTER 4

[UN]BELIEVABLE

THE BIBLE'S PERSPECTIVE ON TODAY'S WORLD

Out Of Sight, Out Of . . . ?

What if, behind all the screens, behind the way they shape our desires, and even behind the designers and media leaders who create them, there is ultimately an unseen, pervasive—yet forgotten—evil?

> *Much that once was is lost, for none now live who remember it.*[90]

As Peter Jackson's epic 2001 theatrical release of Tolkien's *Fellowship of the Ring* opens, Galadriel's hauntingly melodic voice retells the birth of the One Ring.

> *But they were all of them deceived, for another ring was made. In the land of Mordor, in the fires of Mount Doom, the Dark Lord Sauron forged, in secret, a Master Ring to control all others. And into this Ring he poured his cruelty, his malice and his will to dominate all life. One Ring to rule them all.*[91]

We then see the epic battle between Sauron and the combined armies of Middle Earth. Prince Isildur finally cuts the One Ring from the Dark Lord's hand. And yet, the Ring was not destroyed, but was allowed to continue corrupting the hearts of those who found it to be precious.

> And some things that should not have been forgotten were lost. History became legend. Legend became myth. And for two and a half thousand years, the Ring passed out of all knowledge.[92]

Back in the real world, we find ourselves in a similar place. Almost 2,000 years since the events of the New Testament, modern Western culture has largely forgotten the real—yet unseen—spiritual dimension. In fact, regardless of what we say we believe, we often live as if angels, demons, and their battle for the allegiance of mankind is in the same genre as a Tolkien fantasy—fiction.

A big reason we're so blind to spiritual realities is our reverence for atheistic scientists, almost elevating them to the level of a new priesthood. We have accepted the materialistic doctrine that the only "real" things are those things that can be perceived through our five senses. If something can't be seen under a microscope—so they say— it must not actually exist. This strong bias makes many people dismiss the Bible as fiction or myth, since the Scriptures claim unseen spiritual beings are as real as the book you're reading now.

And some atheistic arguments are compelling. Ancient tribes used to think thunder was caused by an angry god, and that doing certain dances or sacrifices would appease him. Scientists later discovered powerful electrostatic charges excited by certain weather patterns, and in so doing, disproved the reality of a "god of thunder." If science has debunked the myths of fairies who make plants grow or angry water-spirits who sink ships, then shouldn't we just go "one god more"[93] as modern atheists do, and completely reject the idea of an unseen spiritual world?

I don't think so. And, since you picked up this book despite the references to biblical practices on the back cover, I'm guessing you're at least open to the Christian worldview that forms the foundation of my identity. After a lifetime of studying the Christian Scriptures, reading atheist literature, and considering many scientific perspectives, I've found that the Bible's worldview most accurately maps to reality—both seen and unseen.[94]

And even if you are a Christian like me, it may take a lot to convince you that there's a spiritual battle for your heart and mind being waged through your devices. You might even be asking yourself, "Really? He's going *there*? He's going to say *the devil* is using screens against us?" It's good to be a little skeptical, but not if you're completely closed off to the truth just because it is unpopular or uncomfortable. I encourage you to hang in there with me while I share what I've learned. Consider my case with an open mind, then decide what you think.

The stakes are huge. If I'm right, we're all being ensnared, immobilized from our true callings, and unable to become what we were made to be because we're distracted and overwhelmed. If we're really being enslaved to our manipulated desires, then we must learn the truth so we can break free.

Dark Trends

But before I "go there," consider: something sinister *is* going on in the world, far beyond our screens. What's more, the Bible anticipated these times, telling us about them thousands of years ago.

People from all walks of life recognize how many cultural trends over the past fifty years aren't taking society to a good place. Perhaps most troubling, suicide has increased in recent years to become the second highest cause of death in the U.S. for people aged 15-34.[95]

The despair that leads to suicide is being fueled by technology. Dr. Jean Twenge coined the term *iGen* for the group of young people who came of age during the release of the iPhone and the iPad. She links the arrival of mobile devices with some very harmful trends. In a recent article in *The Atlantic*, Dr. Twenge wrote, "Rates of teen depression and suicide have skyrocketed since 2011. It's not an exaggeration to describe *iGen* as being on the brink of the worst mental-health crisis in decades. Much of this deterioration can be traced to their phones."[96]

On another note, notice how popular music is taking our thinking—and with it, our culture—to a very dark place. Compare

Billboard's number one song in December 1977[97] with the recording that occupied that same spot in December 2017.[98]

The top song of 1977 was "You Light Up My Life,"[99] popularized by Debby Boone. It drips with sappiness, expressing simple feelings of love without vulgarity, violence, drugs, or sex. Forty years later, the winner was "Rockstar,"[100] by rapper Post Malone. It features at least eight f-bombs to celebrate rape, constant drug use, and the gang-inspired machine-gunning of a neighborhood. I wanted to print the choruses here for you since seeing them side-by-side really tells the story, but because of copyright constraints, I'm not allowed. You can visit the links in the footnotes to read them, if you dare. I feel nauseated when I read Malone's lyrics.

Like the rapid change from *Andy Griffith* to *Game of Thrones* we observed in chapter 3, there is a chilling trajectory to popular media tastes. What kind of society are we becoming if we venerate the values in "Rockstar," where millions of people sing along with lyrics that honor drug-induced sexual violence and murder? The statistics weep as they give us the answer.

In a world where eight-year-olds are exposed to hardcore porn in their own home using a device their parents gave them for Christmas, we need to wonder: how did media and culture *really* get this dark? Could it be that someone unseen, who came to "steal, kill, and destroy" (John 10:10), is very good at achieving his evil goals?

Last Days

When I look at the cultural trends over my lifetime and compare them to what I read in the Bible, I'm amazed at the accuracy of these ancient documents. Some passages are like reading yesterday's news. You'd think the Apostle Paul had recently heard Post Malone when he wrote this:

> But realize this, that in the last days difficult times will come. For men will be lovers of self, lovers of money, boastful, arrogant, revilers, disobedient to parents, ungrateful, unholy, unloving, irreconcilable, malicious gossips,

> without self-control, brutal, haters of good, treacherous, reckless, conceited, lovers of pleasure rather than lovers of God, holding to a form of godliness, although they have denied its power; Avoid such men as these (2 TIMOTHY 3:1–5).

In every age, there have been people with some of these characteristics, but there has never been a time when more people in the world have been exposed to media that inspires *all* of these attributes simultaneously. American popular media is broadcast and streamed constantly to nearly every village on the globe, which means our movie, TV, and music trends are influencing *billions.* A steady diet of *Game of Thrones* and Post Malone are encouraging an entire generation to become the hateful, brutal, reckless, conceited, and pleasure-loving people of Paul's prophesy.

As we noticed in chapter 1, a pervasive sense of mocking, of making fun or turning nearly everything into a flippant and often vulgar joke, is promoted by much of popular media today. Just find a celebrity or political leader on Twitter and look at the comments. In another example of the Bible's reliability, we see the Apostle Peter is not surprised by (anti-)social media.

> Know this first of all, that in the last days mockers will come with their mocking, following after their own lusts, and saying, "Where is the promise of His coming? For ever since the fathers fell asleep, all continues just as it was from the beginning of creation" (2 PETER 3:3–4).

Our current culture ridicules Christian teachings in ways I've never seen before. It's not enough for some non-believers to just disagree; rather, the knee-jerk reaction online is often spiteful, profane, and scornful mocking. In my own dialog with atheists online, I've personally experienced some brutal personal attacks. I am ironically encouraged by such mockers, since I know they are actually fulfilling Peter's prophesy.

As we compare general cultural trends to what the apostles of Jesus predicted about the last days, we see an unmistakable connection. While I'm obviously concerned enough about these changes to write this book, I am also comforted when I see the relevance of the Bible. I recognize that God is ultimately in charge, since he accurately predicted what was going to be happening in our time. He is not surprised or worried. Prophesies like these are one of many reasons to trust the reliability of the Scriptures.

Here's one more prophesy from the Apostle Paul to set up our focus on unseen spiritual forces:

> But the Spirit explicitly says that in later times some will fall away from the faith, paying attention to deceitful spirits and doctrines of demons, by means of the hypocrisy of liars seared in their own conscience as with a branding iron (1 TIMOTHY 4:1–2).

From this verse, it seems even Christ-followers might be deceived so they will fall away, specifically because they are influenced by evil spiritual forces. As we'll see, biblical writers didn't think of spirits and demons as fake or metaphorical. They had first-hand experience battling these unseen forces and, by the grace of God, their writings have been preserved so we can learn from them.

Really Real?

When I introduced the possibility that unseen evil spiritual forces are behind our increasingly immoral, violent, and destructive cultural trajectory, especially through our media, you may have been skeptical. While we might hold a vague hope in guardian angels, most of us don't think seriously about demonic activity. It doesn't help that we've seen devils mocked in horror movies and used as tools of manipulation by TV preachers. All of this makes it hard for us to believe evil spiritual forces are really at work today.

The insightful English author and social critic Os Guinness shows how our culture shuns the idea of spiritual forces in his book *Impossible People*. Guinness writes:

> As theologian Walter Wink observes, "Angels, spirits, principalities, powers, gods, Satan—these, along with other

spiritual realities, are the unmentionables of our culture. The dominant materialistic worldview has absolutely no place for them." They are archaic relics of a primitive past because "modern secularism simply has no categories, no vocabulary, no presuppositions by which to discern what it was in the actual experience of people that brought these words to speech."[101]

Because our culture has "no categories" to discuss spiritual realities such as angels and demons, it defaults to the materialistic dogma that the only reality is what can be seen, and therefore denies them altogether. Few churches raise the unpopular and even scorned subject of spiritual warfare today. Guinness agrees:

> Walter Wink describes demons as the "drunk uncle of the twentieth century: we keep them out of sight." But it is not only demons that embarrass us as sophisticated modern people. So too, it seems, does spiritual warfare and all the teaching and practices that go with it.[102]

Here's a scary thought. What if the fact that modern cultures don't believe in evil spiritual forces is evidence of the success of those very forces? Could their apparent hiddenness be a successful warfare strategy? In human warfare, secret plans are the most devastating, and much effort goes into trying to decode cryptography so armies can learn their enemy's plans. Spiritual forces may very well use even more sophisticated tactics against us.

In *The Screwtape Letters*, C. S. Lewis imagines what goes on behind the scenes when the demons revealed in Scripture make their plans to tempt mankind. The central character is a veteran tempter who is sharing his wisdom with an apprentice. Here's Screwtape's demonic advice about how to influence "the patient"—us:

> I wonder you should ask me whether it is essential to keep the patient in ignorance of your own existence. That question, at least for the present phase of the struggle, has been answered for us by the High Command. Our policy, for the moment, is to conceal ourselves. Of course this

has not always been so. We are really faced with a cruel dilemma. When the humans disbelieve in our existence we lose all the pleasing results of direct terrorism and we make no magicians. On the other hand, when they believe in us, we cannot make them materialists and sceptics. [. . .] I do not think you will have much difficulty in keeping the patient in the dark. The fact that 'devils' are predominantly comic figures in the modern imagination will help you. If any faint suspicion of your existence begins to arise in his mind, suggest to him a picture of something in red tights, and persuade him that since he cannot believe in that (it is an old textbook method of confusing them) he therefore cannot believe in you.[103]

John Wesley warned Christians to beware of what he called "evil angels." He said, "And highly necessary it is that we should well understand what God has revealed concerning [evil angels], that they may gain no advantage over us by our ignorance; that we may know how to wrestle against them effectually."[104] Wesley was right: when we are ignorant of our opponents, they certainly have a huge advantage.

As a Christ-follower, I consider Jesus's thoughts most important as I seek to understand reality. As Andy Stanley points out, if you can predict your own death and resurrection *and* pull it off, you have the credibility to speak with authority on anything else. And Jesus certainly believed and engaged in spiritual warfare.

Before Jesus started his speaking and healing ministry, he went on a 40-day fast in a Middle Eastern wilderness. During that time, he was directly tempted by the devil himself. The first three gospels record the evil one's attempts to lead the Son of God into temptation (Matthew 4, Mark 1, and Luke 4). The writer of Hebrews assures us that, "Jesus was tempted in all things as we are, yet without sin" (Hebrews 4:15), so we can be certain that Satan's temptations were genuinely enticing.

Throughout Jesus's ministry, the gospels show him regularly casting demons out of people who were under their direct influence. In each case, the battle between Jesus and the evil spirit was recorded as historical fact. And here's the best part: Jesus won *every* battle he waged against evil forces. He didn't even seem to break a sweat.

The apostles of Christ also encountered demons and overcame them in the name of Jesus. When Jesus sent seventy disciples on a training mission, they returned saying, "Lord, even the demons are subject to us in Your name" (Luke 10:17). Jesus told them he had given them that authority, but that they shouldn't be too proud (v. 20). After Jesus's ascension, the Apostle Paul had such a powerful ministry of healing and spiritual warfare in Jesus's name that jealous Jewish exorcists tried to imitate Paul. One evil spirit wasn't impressed, but chased these imposters away, saying, "I recognize Jesus, and I know about Paul, but who are you?" (Acts 19:15).

Paul's many battles with demonic forces give him the credibility to write one of the most powerful teachings on spiritual warfare in the Bible—the passage Wesley said, "seems to contain the whole scriptural doctrine concerning evil angels"[105]—in the finale of his letter to the Ephesians.

> For our struggle is not against flesh and blood, but against
> the rulers, against the powers, against the world forces of
> this darkness, against the spiritual forces of wickedness
> in the heavenly places (EPHESIANS 6:12).

Paul was persecuted by hostile religious leaders from the beginning of his ministry. And yet, he tells his readers that humans are never the real enemy. Instead, an unseen, well-organized army of "spiritual forces" is ultimately fighting against us. Paul knew that even though flesh-and-blood humans were making his life difficult, they were—unknowingly—just following unseen orders.

Notice how Paul describes evil spiritual forces in four different ways. There are:

- *rulers* (Greek ἀρχή arché, root of words like architect and archetype), entities at the top of a hierarchy;
- *powers* (Greek ἐξουσία exousia), general authorities or influencers;
- *world forces of this darkness* (Greek κοσμοκράτορας kosmokratoras, you can see 'cosmos' in that compound word), or world-rulers; and

■ *spiritual forces of wickedness* (Greek πνευματικὰ πονηρίας—pneumatika ponērias, the first word the root of pneumatic, also like breath or air), or evil spirits.

These four categories show organization and structure, plus the scope of authority (world-wide) and location (heavenly places). Taken together, these words describe an unseen enemy who is methodical, purposeful, everywhere, immaterial, evil, and actively fighting against us.

Here's the takeaway so far: if we believe the Bible is authoritative, then we *must* believe in the reality of evil spiritual forces. We repeatedly see direct battles between Jesus or his disciples and the forces of the devil recorded as historical events in the New Testament. The broad testimony of engagement in spiritual warfare across the Scriptures is too comprehensive to ignore.

But even if we believe evil spiritual forces are real, how can we know whether they are influencing us personally through our screens and all of the media we consume?

Deceptively Effective

Though the enemy is unseen, we are not left without insight. The link between the negative effects of technology and evil spiritual forces can be known because *the Bible reveals their methods.* By learning the strategies used by spiritual forces to *steal, kill, and destroy* mankind, we can discern whether they are impacting us through our screens. It's like a footprint or DNA sample found at a crime scene—with enough data, an experienced detective can track down the perpetrator.

In a key debate with a group of murderously jealous religious leaders, Jesus, as always, worked like a master surgeon to get to the heart of their animosity. John's gospel tells us these Jews thought they were on higher moral ground because they could trace their lineage back to Abraham. And if that wasn't enough, they further claimed God as their father, asserting a false sense of divine authority to oppose Jesus. But since they were *lying* about Jesus and *deceiving* the crowds, Jesus told them who their father really was, and *how he knew.*

> You are of your father the devil, and you want to do the
> desires of your father. He was a murderer from the begin-
> ning, and does not stand in the truth because there is no
> truth in him. Whenever he speaks a lie, he speaks from his
> own nature, for he is a liar and the father of lies (JOHN 8:44).

According to Jesus, here's the devil's DNA: deception. Jesus says there is no truth in the devil, and even more, he is the *father of lies.* The concept of *father* here is really important. Jesus isn't talking about a physical genealogy, but a bloodline revealed by a pattern of shared behaviors. Wherever you see lies, you can trace them up the family tree, back to their father, the devil. That's how Jesus can so confidently say these liars are children of the evil one.

From the moment the devil slithers onto the pages of Scripture, we hear him lying. In fact, the first lie in the Bible is told by the devil—a further confirmation he is the father of lies. While God warned Adam and Eve that eating from the Tree of the Knowledge of Good and Evil would kill them, the sly serpent told Eve, "You surely will not die" (Genesis 3:4). He goes on to tell Eve she will have God-like powers, implying God is keeping her from obtaining special wisdom and knowledge. As the serpent seductively dangles the beautiful fruit in front of Eve, using the enormous power of distraction to make her forget the truth, she falls for the serpent's craftiness (2 Corinthians 11:3). Then, like an ignorant sheeple, her husband shares in the deadly meal.

The tragic, ironic part of this lie was that Adam and Eve were *already* like God. They were made in his image. And they *already* had the knowledge of good and evil: obedience to God was good, and disobedience was evil. They could have continued learning good and evil directly from God without having to experience the pain, suffering, and death introduced by their disobedience. In the form of a serpent, the devil was able to sidetrack our first parents into forgetting these truths. Distraction turns out to be the sweetener that makes deception so tasty. We forget the truth while we eat the delicious lie. Magicians, con-men, advertisers, and technology leaders know this well.

The Oxford Dictionary chose "post-truth" as the 2016 word of the year. *The Washington Post* declared the news with, "It's official: Truth is dead. Facts are passé."[106] While they were primarily referring to a caustic political climate known for twisting and spinning the truth with the grace of an Olympic ice skater, deception permeates nearly every aspect of our lives. And yes, technology-powered media is the primary source of post-truth content which is intentionally designed to entice us through false messages.

We are so used to slick marketing, airbrushed photos, and too-good-to-be-true deals that we accept them as normal. We aren't surprised to hear we live in a "post-truth" era. We resign ourselves, groaning, "It's just the way it is." And yet, when we start thinking about the number of lies we receive on a daily basis—especially through our screens—the organized, strategic, coordinated effort behind it all becomes obvious. Consider:

- When commercials make you want something you don't really need (and is often bad for you) by precise manipulation of your senses and psychological makeup, they are lying.
- When social media apps foster an urgency to check in, create anxiety about missing out if you don't, and send the message that life is all about you and your "likes," they are lying.
- When violent video game makers claim what you pretend to do doesn't affect your behavior, they are lying.
- When the porn industry says sex is just about you and your pleasure while hiding the physical, mental, emotional, and spiritual consequences, all while claiming to offer you "freedom," they are lying.
- When restaurants precisely engineer their recipes with just the right mix of sugar and salt and fat to be addictive, draw you in with mouth-watering ads that show inedible made-up props photoshopped to look more delicious than possible in real life, then exaggerate healthy attributes and hide unhealthy ones, they are lying.
- When pharmaceutical companies advertise drugs by showing happy people playing on the beach while the voiceover shares horrible and possibly deadly side effects in a soothing voice to pleasant music, they are lying.

- When TV shows portray beautiful and smiling people living immoral lifestyles without any consequences, they are lying.
- When so-called experts supported by big tech companies claim there's no such thing as technology addiction, they are lying.
- When other experts claim more technology is beneficial to children, they are lying.
- When still more experts let adults off the hook with their technology obsessions by only focusing on the negative effects on children, they are lying.
- When pictures of photoshopped women set an unachievable standard of beauty while turning women into sex objects, they are lying.
- When a web site or email creates false scarcity by urging you to act now or miss out on the deal of your life, they are lying.
- When media companies secretly collect volumes of your personal data while hiding their intentions behind unreadable terms and conditions, they are lying.
- When anyone says you should do whatever makes you feel good because that's where happiness comes from, they are lying.
- When the makers of music videos glamorize rape, violence, and drugs and claim what we listen to doesn't affect our behavior, they are lying.

To be clear, as I share this short summary of cultural lies, I'm not claiming that in every case the people involved are *intending to lie* or they know what they are doing is deceptive (though many do). I'm simply saying that in each of these examples, someone is promoting a lie, whether they know it or not. And where there are lies, we can trace them back to their source—the unseen father of lies who has been practicing his art of deception for at least as long as there have been people on earth.

Also notice, as we saw earlier, all of these deceptions lead to harmful outcomes. All the trends they create are going in the wrong direction. It's not as though the messages we are receiving through addictive, desire-shaping screens are compelling us to be more loving, selfless, generous, wise, peaceful, or gracious. If that were the case, we might not be so concerned. But they are leading many people to the opposite: less love, joy, peace, patience, kindness, goodness, faithfulness, gentleness, meekness, and certainly less self-control (Galatians 5:22). This is further evidence that evil spiritual forces are behind much of today's media. The outcomes are what we would expect from someone who is always prowling "like a roaring lion, seeking someone to devour" (1 Peter 5:8).

But does the devil really have this kind of power? What kind of authority, organization, strength, or influence would it take to literally be the father of every lie? Especially lies that are propagated through technology on a scale humanity has never seen before?

Worldwide Power

The Bible is full of powerful declarations that show the global influence of the devil and his spiritual forces. Consider:

> We know that we are of God, and that the **whole world lies in the power of the evil one** (1 JOHN 5:19, emphasis mine).

> And you were dead in your trespasses and sins, in which you formerly walked according to the course of this world, according to the **prince of the power of the air**, of the spirit that is now working in the sons of disobedience (EPHESIANS 2:1–2, emphasis mine).

> And even if our gospel is veiled, it is veiled to those who are perishing, in whose case the **god of this world** has blinded the minds of the unbelieving so that they might not see the light of the gospel of the glory of Christ, who is the image of God (2 CORINTHIANS 4:3–4, emphasis mine).

> And the great dragon was thrown down, the serpent of old who is called the devil and Satan, **who deceives the whole world**; he was thrown down to the earth, and his angels were thrown down with him (REVELATION 12:9, emphasis mine).

When Jesus was tempted by Satan in Luke 4, the devil showed Jesus "all the kingdoms of the world," claiming they had "been handed over to me [the devil], and I give [them] to whomever I wish" (Luke 4:5-6). Jesus doesn't challenge Satan's claim. Apparently, the devil has a significant amount of authority over the world. Thankfully, his authority is limited, restrained, and coming to an end, as Revelation 12 declares.

But for now, these verses share a disturbing theme. The devil has power and authority over the entire world, as a prince, even a "god." The work of his global organization is to deceive everyone on the planet, 24x7x365. Albert Barnes, the 19th-century Christian theologian and minister, agrees in his insightful Bible commentary:

> [The devil] secured the apostasy of man, and early brought him to follow his plans; and he has maintained his scepter and dominion since. No more abject submission could be desired by him than has been rendered by the mass of people.[107]

In his more formal language, Barnes says the widespread devotion of mankind to the devil's ways is evidence of his authority and power. As he "secured the apostasy" or tricked our first parents into disobeying God in the Garden of Eden, so he now maintains his evil rule over those who will follow him on the earth. The evil one keeps his power and position using the same deceptive methods that have always worked for him. Barnes continues:

> The dominion of Satan over this world has been, and is still almost universal and absolute; nor has the lapse of 1,800 years rendered the appellation improper as descriptive of his influence, that he is the god of this world [translation: Satan hasn't lost any power or authority since the New Testament was written.]. The world pursues his plans; yields to his temptations; neglects, or rejects the reign of God as he pleases; and submits to his scepter, and is still full of abomination, cruelty, and pollution, as he desires it to be.[108]

The fact of Satan's rule is shown by his worldwide influence, how so much of mankind willingly marches to his drumbeat. We can know spiritual forces have global power by observing their effects. Barnes confirms the ongoing effectiveness of Satan's power, and shows how we can recognize the devil's influence by simple observation.

I find the "prince of the power of the air" (Ephesians 2:2) a particularly interesting phrase, since most of today's deceptions are literally carried by digital signals transmitted through the air. When Paul wrote this phrase, there were no human-generated airborne electronic signals; today, we are permeated by them. I wonder if the "spiritual forces of wickedness in the heavenly places" love the irony (Ephesians 6:12).

Believing the Unbelievable

There really are evil spiritual forces. We see their fingerprints everywhere. The Bible confirms the negative cultural trends we see and blames them on demonic influences. We know deception is the primary strategy of the evil one. Because of Jesus's declaration that Satan is the "father of lies," we know wherever we see falsehood, evil spiritual forces are ultimately responsible. Deception fills the screen-based messages that are intentionally crafted to shape our desires. Therefore, we can confidently link our distractions, compulsions, addictions, and all of the other ways we are pulled away from our God-given purpose to the "prince of the power of the air." Os Guinness agrees, saying:

> In, behind and above titanic powers such as human empires and ideologies, there are dark supernatural powers at work and opposed to the kingdom of our Lord. **We will never explain reality or prevail against the opposition if we engage only on the natural plane of reality.** There is not only an unseen world beyond the seen, but time and again the real battle is in the unseen world— a war in heaven. Those who win the battle in the heavens are the decisive factor in the course of history.[109]

As we wrap up this chapter, consider Jesus's warning from the earlier debate with deceitful religious leaders:

> But because I speak the truth, you do not believe Me. [. . .]
> He who is of God hears the words of God; for this reason
> you do not hear them, because you are not of God (JOHN
> 8:45, 47).

If people are immersed in lies long enough, they lose the capacity to hear what is true. Their minds are so warped by deception they can't perceive God's truths anymore. I think this is why "the father of lies" works so hard to deceive us every moment of the day. After a diet of constant lies, many people become unable to receive the truth that would set them free (John 8:32).

What a fearful thought! We can be so saturated in deception that we literally cannot hear truth. We can become so used to hearing lies that the truth is like a foreign language—incomprehensible. And screens are so good at holding our attention and establishing the categories of what we accept as "real" that biblical truth hardly stands a chance.

The truths I've learned and shared here are too important to ignore. The enemy would have us stay distracted, make no changes, and continue to follow his desires for us, which will ultimately lead to our demise. His methods have been working for millennia, and as we've seen, they've never been more effective.

We can only begin to imagine what is being lost on a global scale as the result of the enemy's colossal success at deceiving us. How many creative people—individuals who could be thinking of the next breakthrough solutions to many of the world's greatest problems—are instead so distracted and anxious and filled with lies they can't begin to consider what their potential impact could be? What diseases could have been cured by now? How many lives made better by advances in technologies to clean air and water? How many poverty-stricken people might already have been lifted from their hopelessness by innovative agricultural techniques or entrepreneurially focused business opportunities?

How many people are being led into lives they will always regret because they are following the ever-present cultural lies propagated by the evil one? How many young girls are lured into the sex trade because they believe that's what they're made for, or that being a sex object is the best they can do? How many young boys are twisted in their minds because of porn? How many people can't even imagine a world filled with goodness, truth, hope, joy, or light because of the darkness they constantly receive through their games, movies, music, and social media?

Worst of all, how many people are unable to comprehend God's call to them through Jesus Christ because they can't imagine the possibility of a good God somewhere beyond the noise and clutter and near-madness generated by constant exposure to screens?

If you're being pulled away from the life God made you to live by an unseen but very real enemy, how does that make you feel? From what you've read so far, do you think it is possible you're being led off track into various addictions because of an evil spiritual agenda bent on your destruction? If so, what are you willing to do in response?

For me, the knowledge of these truths motivates me to seek God's truth and take action. If there's a spiritual root to our problems, then the answers, the response, and the freedom we can experience are also spiritual. If we're going to break free from the devil's influence, God is going to have to empower us.

We now see how *some things that should not have been forgotten* can be *lost.* Thankfully, the Bible promises that those who follow Christ have the power to walk in a freedom that overcomes the lies of the evil one. The practices we'll learn in coming chapters are all focused on helping us to find this freedom in Christ. Now that you've learned the depth of the malicious intentionality aimed against you, I hope you'll continue with me while we learn together how to find and live the overcoming life God has promised, even in today's screen-saturated world.

CHAPTER 5

[UN]EVALUATED

A PROCESS FOR MEASURING EXACTLY WHERE YOU ARE

Asking the Question

"Who am I, Gamling?"

King Théoden of Rohan asks this piercing question of his trusted armor-bearer as more than 10,000 gigantic, muscle-bound, and hideous warriors march against his mountain fortress. His handful of fighting men, most of whom had "seen too many winters, or too few," were no match force-on-force against the hateful monsters who were bred to annihilate mankind. As the king prepares to lead his people into this hopeless battle, the moment overwhelms him, and he questions himself, his leadership, and his life.

Gamling reminds him, "You are our king, sire, and your men will follow you to whatever end." As Théoden processes the dire moment in the climactic ending of Tolkien's *The Two Towers*, he ends his searching and doubt-filled dialog with this haunting question:

"How did it come to this?"

It's time for us to ask similar questions after what we've learned in the last four chapters. In fact, after hearing about all of the forces marching against us, you might be feeling a little (or a lot) over-whelmed, like the battle is too much for you to handle. I feel that way sometimes. My heart breaks and my mind spins as I consider the mag-nitude of the problems: screens everywhere, their messages, the de-sire-manipulating and intentionally addictive strategies, the negative changes to society as a result, and especially the lives being torn apart and wasted—all because the individuals were unable to overcome the many forces aimed at their destruction.

But I wouldn't have written this book if there wasn't hope—if there wasn't a way to live in freedom and purpose even in the face of Tolkien-epic-sized opposition.

Before you can know what you need to do to overcome whatever is keeping you from all you were made to become, you need a clear picture of where you are right now. That's the purpose of this chapter; to help you ask the question: *Who am I, really?* By carefully evaluating your life, you'll be able to see what you may need to change so that you can live the life you are called to live.

But first, let's quickly review what we've covered. Chapter 1 in-creased our awareness to the pervasiveness and impact of screens—the tidal wave that has flooded the whole world with distraction, uncivil discourse, mocking, sexualization, and the inability to think deeply. Chapter 2 highlighted the intentionally desire-shaping and often addicting strategies used by media elites, along with their in-sidious double-bind: they encourage us to do whatever *we* feel or de-sire, then manipulate us to feel and desire what is most profitable to *them.* Chapter 3 introduced us to the people and companies behind these strategies, who, motivated by an unprincipled hunger for power and profit, masterfully leverage early 20th-century propaganda tech-niques through our screens. Finally, chapter 4 revealed the unseen but very real and evil spiritual forces who are really behind the ef-forts to deceive and enslave humanity through the intentional manip-ulation of our desires.

I've painted a pretty bleak picture, not unlike the onslaught faced by Tolkien's king Théoden. I wanted you to see clearly that the battle is real, huge, and affects everyone. So, now what? What can anyone do against such overwhelming, pervasive, and world-dominating forces?

This chapter seeks to help us answer this question by evaluating the only thing in the world we have control over: ourselves. We can't begin to change the world until we understand how the world is changing us. I'm sure as you've been reading and considering these things, you may have even started to think about your own relationship with screens.

And in your considering, you may have started to feel shame—maybe for the first time. If that's you, I want to encourage you not to go there. None of what I've shared is intended to shame anyone (except maybe those who intentionally manipulate the rest of us). You *may* need to make some changes, but shaming yourself isn't going to lead you in a positive direction. A cycle of self-shaming only keeps you ensnared and hopeless, and is powered by another lie from the father of lies. The evil one will encourage self-shaming to keep you stuck in self-destructive behaviors. The truth is, we all have areas in our lives we need to improve.

Even if you're involved in behaviors the Bible calls sinful—if you're watching porn or other immoral content, if you're gambling, or envying, or compulsively gaming, or overspending—self-shaming isn't going to move you forward. I *definitely* want you to take those things very seriously, as God does, because he loves you. That's why he hates it when we harm ourselves or others. Ultimately, I want you to be free from anything that enslaves you. I know you can be free— if you're willing to directly confront any sinful behaviors, instead of pushing them aside, ignoring them, excusing them, or becoming so hopeless you remain ensnared.

And I've been there. When I was involved with porn many years ago, I remember the shame, the guilt over my sin, and yet the pull of selfish pleasure fueled by the growing availability of more. I know what it feels like to be so ashamed and hopeless that "I may as well just give in," because I feel like I'm worthless, I've gone too far, and I'm powerless to overcome. And yet, standing on this side of many years of freedom, I can tell you with confident hope that in Christ, you can find freedom from anything that is keeping you enslaved.

The Right Posture

On the plus side, you're taking positive steps by continuing to read a book that was specifically written to help you overcome. You're seeking advice, or you're at least curious enough to explore whether change is possible. That's a huge reason to be hopeful and to put shame aside while you begin to take a serious look at yourself and the impact technology is really having on you.

Continuing on this line of thinking, here are six positive "postures of evaluation." I want to encourage you to keep these in mind as you begin to survey your life. Without the right posture, it will be very difficult to see a clear picture of where you are. You wouldn't still be hanging in there with me if you weren't seeking clarity. If you adopt these traits, you'll be well prepared to do a helpful and productive self-evaluation.

1. **Grace**. The first posture of evaluation is to look at ourselves through the gracious eyes of our Heavenly Father. He sees us through lenses of love, even when he is angry at our sinful ways (John 3:16). In fact, the Bible says, "the kindness of God leads [us] to repentance" (Romans 2:4b). By adopting this posture, we decide to agree with God's attitude toward us. If he can be gracious to us, giving us time to identify and turn away (repent) from what is harming us or others, then we can be gracious with ourselves.

2. **Patience**. Our present behaviors, habits, practices, attitudes, and possibly manipulated desires weren't formed overnight. Where we are today is the result of many small, incremental decisions over the course of months or years. Because it took time to get here, any lasting change will take time too. That's not to say that God can't change people immediately, radically, and completely—he has, and he can. But more often, it seems God uses the strategies of a patient farmer, alternately pruning unfruitful branches and allowing fruitful branches to grow at their own pace (John 15:1-5).

3. **Objectivity**. From a posture of grace and patience, we can take a more objective view of ourselves. This means we look at ourselves like we would look at anyone else we cared about and truly wanted to help. Without an impartial lens toward ourselves, it's easy to alternate

between making excuses or beating ourselves down. Neither of these lines of thought are helpful. Instead, it is very powerful to look at ourselves as though we were a dear friend. We can offer a more accurate perspective to a close friend because we aren't personally affected by what they choose to do with our advice. The more neutral, fair, unbiased, and even clinical we can be as we look at ourselves, the more accurate and helpful our evaluation will be.

4. **Openness**. A cousin of objectivity, a posture of openness will make it more likely that you'll clearly see what needs to be seen. If you're unwilling to ask certain questions or if you have pet habits that are off-limits, you won't learn what you really need to learn as you evaluate yourself. Don't be afraid of what you may learn. Only those who have no secrets from God and from those who are closest to them are truly free anyway. The fact is, we've all done things we're ashamed of, and "pobody's nerfect." People are typically closed to learning about needed areas of change when they're afraid of looking flawed to others. But those who will see the greatest positive results from evaluation are those who are most open to whatever needs to be learned.

5. **Optimism**. As you see things in your life that need to change, it's easy to be pessimistic, especially if you learn unflattering things about yourself. But a negative attitude can be a weapon of spiritual warfare used by your enemy to hold you back. Instead, remember positive truths all along the way. Trust that God truly loves you (Romans 5:8), he wants your good (Romans 8:28), and he is going to help you (Psalm 46:1). Believe that he will give you the light you need (John 8:12) and the strength to do what needs to be done with the light you receive (2 Peter 1:3-4). Know that he has promised never to leave you or forsake you (Hebrews 13:5b).

6. **Restraint**. The posture of restraint is less intuitive, but still vital. When you see the impact that screens are having on your life, you might be tempted to make immediate changes. It's good that you want to change, but impulsive changes can, unfortunately, lead to worse outcomes. You might decide to cut back or stop something right away, only to find yourself back at it a few days later, leading to deeper discouragement. Addictions are powerful, and overcoming them requires God's power and our wise cooperation with him. Few fad diets

or New Year's resolutions make a lifelong difference. Just take note of things you may want to change and start thinking and praying about them, but hold yourself back from taking significant action—at least until you reach the later chapters of this book. Note: This posture isn't an excuse to go and indulge in something you know is wrong. Don't do that. The idea is to be strategic in your future changes so that they'll really stick, because they are grounded in wisdom and empowered by God.

A Dangerous Prayer

The late 18th/early 19th-century poet, philosopher, and theologian Samuel Taylor Coleridge said, "There is one art of which every man should be a master—the art of reflection. If you are not a thinking man, to what purpose are you a man at all?"[110] Of course, all women and men are created by God to become wise, careful, reflective, and insightful thinkers. Though you might not consider yourself introspective, evaluation is an act of self-learning, so it is introspective by definition. And Coleridge says there is an art to reflection, and part of our God-given purpose is to get really good at it.

The posture of Openness is an especially critical aspect of the art of reflection. To be most effective, our openness must be directed toward the One who knows us best and who can be most helpful in not only teaching us what we need to learn, but in helping us overcome. Psalm 139 is a model of a particularly dangerous prayer of openness before the Almighty.

> O Lord, You have searched me and known me.
> You know when I sit down and when I rise up;
> You understand my thought from afar.
> You scrutinize my path and my lying down,
> And are intimately acquainted with all my ways....
> Where can I go from Your Spirit?
> Or where can I flee from Your presence?
> If I ascend to heaven, You are there;
> If I make my bed in Sheol, behold, You are there....

Search me, O God, and know my heart;
Try me and know my anxious thoughts;
And see if there be any hurtful [wicked / offensive /
grievous] way in me,
And lead me in the everlasting way

(PSALM 139:1–3, 7–8, 23–24).

Considering these powerful truths can lead you to a new openness you may never have known before. God knows us completely—better than anyone else knows us. He already has "searched and known" us (v. 1). He knows more about us than any big-data-collecting cloud-based technology behemoth will ever know. God knows us *intimately.* There's nowhere we can go where he isn't present.

The last four lines of the psalm (vv. 23-24) feel a little dangerous—they're risky, so they can make us feel vulnerable. Even though God has already searched and known us, our openness to invite him to search and know us more means we're giving him permission to tell us anything, no matter how hard it is for us to hear. Declaring our willingness to let God find any hurtful behavior or thought is very brave, since with our invitation, God *will* do it. This is a prayer he *will* answer, perhaps in unexpected ways.

Being our loving Heavenly Father, God not only answers this prayer, but he also answers it with grace. He won't tell us more about ourselves than we can handle right now. As a result, I find this to be a prayer I must pray on a regular basis. It seems that after God shows me something I need to change and helps me to eventually overcome it, he then graciously reveals a new opportunity for me to grow and improve. Since God knows we can become overwhelmed and discouraged when we think there is too much wrong with us, he will typically tell us only what we need to know today.

I encourage you to join me in praying this prayer even now. If you can take even a few minutes to have a one-on-one with God, go to a quiet place, and with an open and willing heart, pray through these words from Psalm 139. You might even want to bring something to write on (maybe not electronic) so you can record what you learn and begin to consider—to reflect—on what you see. If nothing earth-shattering happens this first time, don't be discouraged. Remember, a good posture of evaluation is gracious, patient, and optimistic. With time and practice, this prayer will be answered.

Many people's lives are so filled with media that the idea of being quiet before God for even a few minutes is daunting. I believe the enemy of our souls keeps our lives filled with noise so that we cannot hear what our Maker would say to us. With a constant stream of messages from elsewhere, we don't notice that we're missing the one Messenger we need more than any other.

If you are in the habit of always having constant input—a speaker in the shower, sleeping with your phone—then taking time to be quiet before God may cause quite a bit of anxiety. I know how that feels. You might try for a few seconds of quiet and find yourself getting distracted. That's OK. Like a muscle that hasn't been used for a long time, it will take time to build up the strength to be silent before God. You might only be able to do "reps" of 30 seconds, then one minute, then five. As before, adopt a posture of grace, patience, and optimism with yourself. Don't give up. The truth you'll learn from your Heavenly Father is worth putting aside the constant stream of lies that aren't taking you where you really want to go anyway.

Addiction

The word "addiction" is thrown around in society in the same nonchalant way that "bingeing" has become acceptable when talking about spending hours watching the latest show. As a result, the seriousness of bona-fide addictions is sometimes minimized and even joked about. But anyone who has been close to an addict knows it's anything but funny.

Alcoholism is an addiction that destroys many thousands of lives. Recovery processes are so well known, people make fun of Alcoholics Anonymous meetings. Even the sharks in Pixar's *Finding Nemo* engaged in a "meeting" where they introduced themselves and confessed their struggle with an "addiction" to eating fish. The success of AA's twelve steps in the lives of many gives them the last laugh over those who don't know the power of the addiction or the joy of recovery.

One common attribute shared by most addicts before they become open to change is *denial*. Most addicts in the bondage of their addiction lie to themselves about it—it's not that serious, it doesn't really hurt anything, they can handle it, or they don't really need to change anything. When their close friends or loved ones mention something about the problem, they often deny it or become defensive.

Stories of recovered alcoholics are always inspiring, and often begin with them hitting some kind of low point where they recognize how much their drinking was costing them. They lose jobs, marriages, money, and health as the "demon in the bottle" has its way. As they begin recovery, they accept the truth of their addiction and stop denying it.

Here's the thing: if you're one of the growing throng of people who are truly addicted to a screen, you might still be in the denial phase. You may have breezed through the posture of evaluation and Psalm 139 without anything sticking, all while hiding the fact that you're playing video games every night instead of sleeping, that every time you're alone you go back to porn, or you compulsively check Instagram dozens of times a day. You may simply not be ready to accept the truth that you have a problem. Until you're willing to take that step, no solution will present itself. Nothing will help you until you open yourself to the idea that you really are addicted and you need help.

As you see results of the upcoming tests and monitoring tools, you might learn that you really are addicted after all. If you do discover an addiction, know that you might need to open yourself up to outside help. Every recovered addict knows the road to recovery begins with this admission: I have a problem, it's too big for me to handle, and I'm going to need help to break free. If that's you, I want to encourage you in your path, and invite you to open yourself to the possibility of a wonderful new life of freedom.

Or, someone close to you may be in denial about their screen addiction. They may be as clueless about their compulsion as it is obvious to you. You might be reading this in hope of finding help for them. If so, I encourage you to learn as much as you can, but recognize that as with any other addiction, you can't nag or complain or guilt anyone into changing. Denial is a powerful force field around those who aren't ready to admit the truth. The complaints of those around them sometimes come off as self-righteous, holier-than-thou statements of people who don't really know or understand.

Often, the pain you feel comes from the loss of valid needs you want your addicted loved one to meet. They spend more time with their screen than with you. They spend money they don't have to admire their addiction instead of admiring you. You feel lonely, and your loneliness can sometimes lead to a justification for grumbling.

It's not easy, for sure, but your posture of evaluation needs to be focused on yourself more than on evaluating the person you're worried about. You need to make sure your heart is in a place of grace, patience, objectivity, openness, optimism and restraint, not only toward yourself, but toward your loved one as well. Recognize your inability to change the other person. Find a community of people where you can receive healthy and helpful support. Pray and trust God to make any needed changes. And in the meantime, trust God to meet the needs that are not being met by your addicted loved one.

Gathering the Data

Much of our identity—who we really are—is revealed by the way we spend our time. Because our time reflects our real life, we need an accurate view of how much time we're spending on our screens and what we're doing when we use them. Only then will we know who we really are and are becoming.

Apps

If you already suspect that your phone is consuming more of your life than it should, or if others have suggested that to you, then perhaps the first step is to find out if that's really the case. Nothing reveals the unknown like real live data. Like your savings account balance tells you what kind of saver you are, your actual time spent using your phone will uncover your true relationship with it.

Since "screen time" is such a hot topic, there are many apps available that track activity: time on the device; the number of times you've checked it; which apps you're using and for how long; and how your usage compares to others. You can go to your Apple or Google app store to find one. Two top-rated monitoring apps are Moment for iOS, and QualityTime for Android. And since iOS version 12, Apple devices have a built-in "Screen Time" feature that will also monitor your usage.

Regardless of the tool you choose, track your typical device usage for at least a couple of weeks. While it will be hard not to make any changes, try to forget you're being tracked. You want an honest assessment. If you don't do what you usually do, then you won't know the truth. You don't mis-calibrate the scale before you step on if you want to know your actual weight. There's no reason to hide from reality, and plenty of reasons not to. With a posture of objectivity, you can read your usage stats like you were evaluating anyone else.

Other Screens

If your computer or game console is a bigger part of your life, you'll need to find a way to track that time, even though it won't be automatic. It's easy to start a daily log—either on a real paper notepad, or a note-taking app. A simple table with the date, time started, time ended, and primary activity will tell the story. Again, track real usage, and don't change anything yet. Get an accurate picture. If you're gaming ten hours a day, then you need to know that. If that information makes you want to change, all the better, but this isn't the time for making that change. This is the time for learning. Just gather data.

You need to know what effect other screens are having on you as well. I encourage you to use the same daily log for any TV or other video watching you do. This is actually the same method the TV rating systems used before computer days; selected families kept a diary of the shows they watched and physically mailed them in. You can do the same thing, and after a while, you'll just get used to it. You'll become less self-conscious. Remember, you're like an objective scientist, studying a subject in its native habitat, just curious as to how it behaves.

After a few weeks of tracking all of your screens, summarize the data. How many hours a day, week, month, and year do you spend on screens? The average is over 30 hours a week, almost the length of a full-time job. If you're unhappy about your number, good! Use that feeling to begin to motivate you to seek the change you're looking for.

But not yet—be patient, meditate on what you've learned, and remember how it makes you feel.

Questionnaires

There are many online tests that assess the presence and intensity of addictive behaviors. One of my favorite places to find them is Families Managing Media (FMM). This non-profit organization was founded by Melanie Hempe, a mom who raised her son Adam with no restraints on his video game usage. He became an addict. After learning of the reality and impact of her son's addiction, Hempe founded FMM to help other parents protect their kids from similar problems. She has published several surveys focused on children, since that's her mission. You can go to http://www.familiesmanagingmedia.com to see whether your child is addicted to video games, social media, or other screens. It's really important for all parents to truly *parent* their kids, and I don't know an organization that is more focused on that mission.

But my focus is more on adults like you and me, since we are just as susceptible to addiction as are kids, and we're more prone to denial. Sure, a child's brain is much more malleable, so the effects of screen addictions are worse for them. But grown-ups too often excuse themselves, thinking "I'm an adult, I can do what I want," all while wasting as much or more of their lives as the stereotypical teen who spends all her time in her room staring at her phone.

Psychologist Dr. Kimberly Young is a pioneer in the research and treatment of internet addiction, having studied the subject since 1995. She was motivated when a friend asked for help with her husband who at that time was spending 40-60 hours a week in AOL chat rooms.[111] She developed an Internet Addiction Test by copying a compulsive gambling assessment and substituting the word "internet" for "gambling." She found that even in those early days of online usage (anyone remember modems?), people were already showing signs of true addiction.

I encourage you to visit Dr. Young's site at http://netaddiction.com and take her 20-question test. You'll receive a score on a standardized scale that will help you see whether you have a more clinically defined addiction. You can substitute the word "smartphone" or "game" or "TV" or whatever other device for "internet" or "online" in the survey. As before, answer objectively and truthfully so you'll see the accurate picture you need to change your life.

If you take the test and are concerned about your score, good! You may never have considered some of these questions, and are taking the first steps of freedom to live the life you were made to live.

There are several other online tools for assessing various screen addictions. Professor Gijsbert Stoet has created a collection of them at his PsyToolkit site (http://psytoolkit.org). He provides tests for "problematic internet use," social media addiction, and several others. If you're looking for more insight, I encourage you to try some of his assessments to see what more you can learn about where you are right now.

If you want to take these tests to another level, I encourage you to ask someone close to you—someone who would know how you really live—to answer these questions with you. Discuss them with your spouse or significant other, or with a trusted mentor. With a posture of openness, decide that you are willing to hear what may be difficult, because you're willing to learn the truth in order to be set free.

Deeper Questions

As part of becoming more intentional about your screen usage, you might have expected to do some tracking and tests like I've shared, and rightly so. The things you learn from these provide a good baseline. But I want to encourage you to go even deeper. My contention throughout this book is that screens are shaping our desires to make us want things that are taking us away from the lives we were created to live. If that's true, then we need to figure out which of our desires aren't good for us, and where they are leading us.

The tricky thing is that our desires are *ours*. Right now, we want what we want, regardless of why we want it. Whether the desire was implanted by hours or years of exposure to desire-manipulating messages, or whether they are in-born, it doesn't matter—we want what we want. What is critical is to parse the difference between what we want and what we *really* or *ultimately* want.

As Andy Stanley often says, "direction, not intention, determines destination." It doesn't matter if you're in Nebraska and *want* to drive to Oregon, you'll never get there if you go east. No matter how passionately and wholeheartedly you *want* to see the Pacific coast, if you keep driving toward the Atlantic, you'll drive into it before you ever see the Pacific shores. And if you *really* want to go west but something is intentionally enticing you to go east instead, wouldn't you want to find out how and why?

To learn whether your desires are taking you where you *really* want to go, you need to evaluate the path you've taken to bring you to this point in your life. Are your key relationships healthy? Are you serving the kids in your life well? How are your finances? Is your career on track? How about your physical health—are you where you hoped to be at this point in your life? And what about your relationship with God—are you firmly committed to him and his ways and walking in daily closeness with him?

If you're not happy with the answer to any of these questions, then start asking more questions. How did you get to this place? What behaviors are keeping you from better outcomes? And what role do screens have in making you *want* to do the things that are pulling you away from these important priorities? Are the things you *want* to do keeping you from what you *really* believe is most important? If so, it is very likely that your desires have been shaped by those external forces, and you've been unintentionally following those desires to the unhappy path you have identified. Matthew Kelly, author of *Perfectly Yourself*, says, "sometimes long-term misery comes disguised as short-term pleasure."[112]

Again, these are great questions to explore with a trusted family member, friend, or mentor. You may even want to hire a life coach— something I've done in the past that, in part, led me to write this book. The dialog with someone who knows you and can, most importantly, speak the truth to you in love, will enable you to see clearly and form the most effective starting place for positive change.

Here's the vital truth I want everyone to hear clearly. *Our desires aren't the most important part of who we are, and they don't form our identity. As a result, our harmful desires can be changed.* If you're like me, you can think back to things you used to like that you don't like anymore. Maybe there were things you did as a child that seemed good at the time, but you stopped doing them a long time ago. Perhaps you've made positive changes in your health or your work ethic, and your life is better as a result. Those are all changes in *desire*: proof that *what we want right now doesn't define who we are.*

Isn't this great news? Your desires can change! If what you want isn't good for you, you aren't stuck. It's hard—sometimes really, really hard—to change our desires, especially where habits or addictions are involved. But even addicts who recover find that their addiction didn't define their identity. The clear distinction between *who we are* and *what we want* is a critical factor to consider as we pursue a life of freedom.

How Did It Come To This?

Like King Théoden, after evaluating where you are and where you wish you were, you might be asking this hard question: *How did it come to this?* You might feel as discouraged as he was when facing 10,000 monsters all bent on destroying everything he loved.

But Théoden's first question is much more important and productive when asked with the good posture we've learned. Asking *"Who am I?"* can both open new possibilities and form critical boundaries. As you consider, measure, and assess your time and desires, you can decide what to do with what you are learning through your deepening process of self-evaluation. And, if you don't like who you have become, knowing that change is possible brings much hope.

Matthew Kelly says, "Who you are today is only a shadow of who you are capable of being. It is our potential that most excites and frustrates us."[113] When you ask, "Who am I?" you may feel excitement about what is possible and frustration at your lack of progress. I've felt both. The postures of grace and optimism will help you see that your past doesn't define you; rather, it teaches you. Your Heavenly Father has given you the desire to be who he created you to be, and he's also given you the ability to grow as you trust and follow him. As a result, your potential is much greater than you can imagine.

That's why the next chapter is all about casting a vision for what is possible, and what is so desperately needed, in your own life. Before you can really overcome what you need to overcome, you need a better reason than "I shouldn't do that because it's bad for me." You need positive motivation. We all do. We don't say "no" to anything that brings a short-term pleasure unless there is a better "yes" that we know about and can focus on. Discovering your better "yes" will inspire and empower you to continue growing into the intentional person you were made to be.

CHAPTER 6

[UN]ANTICIPATED

CASTING A VISION OF YOUR INTENTIONAL FUTURE

To Die For

"You're going to have to kill me!"

Drenched, disoriented, and holding on for his life, Truman pilots his small sailboat to escape the comfortable—yet false—life he has lived on an island-sized TV studio. *The Truman Show's* director, with god-like power over the island, commands a huge windstorm, complete with lightning strikes, in an attempt to capsize the uncooperative star. With a defiant cry, Truman proclaims his willingness to die for his freedom. He had learned his whole world was nothing but an elaborate plot designed to keep him making more episodes for the benefit of the advertisers. That knowledge propelled him to find a truly authentic life, even if he had to sacrifice everything in the search.

We are surrounded by technologies that are intentionally used to manipulate our desires and lead us away from the lives we were created to live. If we're going to get back on course, we're going to need Truman-like determination. It will take a relentless willingness to sail against the winds of a culture that threatens to sink every person who dares to seek the truth, instead of giving in to the lies communicated on nearly every screen. This kind of determination starts with a clear vision—a "why"—an anticipation of what can be done, while also pursuing a profoundly counter-cultural life.

But where does a vision strong enough to really inspire us come from?

It doesn't come from a screen. It doesn't come from news channels designed to keep us all anxious about the crisis *du jour*, as they divide society into quarreling and ineffective factions. It doesn't come from social media, where truth is never as trendy as the latest celebrity gossip or scandal. It doesn't come from commercials, which sell us quick fixes to the very problems they create in our minds. Virtually every message is designed for one thing: to keep us wanting and consuming more of *their* vision for our lives. As Rod Dreher shares in an article by Charlie Clark:

> The mass of humanity is intentionally kept sunk in everydayness. Absent a direct confrontation with the malaise, the main business of life for most people becomes maintaining a subjective sense of wellbeing, however tenuous, by satisfying the body's felt needs and keeping the mind distracted. In such a society, power and authority are accorded to the scientists, technicians, and other experts who help keep ordinary people content through therapeutic conditioning, helping them adjust to an essentially animal existence.[114]

When most people take a few quiet moments to think outside the "essentially animal existence" of running here and there while staring at screens, they often feel dissatisfied. But more distractions are ever-present, so they are ready targets for the next fast food commercial or social media notification or one-click purchase—whatever provides the "therapeutic conditioning" needed to cover up the fleeting feeling of uneasiness.

The Assault on Vision

Distraction is the arch-enemy of vision. If we're going to accomplish anything worthwhile, we must have a vision for what could possibly be done. But with constant distractions, we are unable to even start to consider a vision beyond the next five seconds. We can't know what the world really needs from us or what God may be calling us to do if we're constantly blinded by the next tweet, commercial, show, or billboard. We can't even know our own thoughts.

The inability to think clearly caused by ubiquitous screen-enhanced noise is like driving in the dark through a thick fog. Our imagination has no room for a positive future, because the future is completely hidden. That's why our enemy works so hard to keep us distracted. His objective—to "steal, kill, or destroy" our future—is super easy for him these days. All he has to do is keep us thinking about something—anything—besides the positive future God is calling us to live.

If distraction doesn't completely cloud our vision, then the enemy deploys the weapon of hopelessness. In those rare, quiet moments when we escape all screens and feel dissatisfied with where we are, or we see problems in the world and we want to help, then those self-defeating thoughts flood our minds. "There's nothing I can do," or, "this is just the way life is," or, "I'll never be [strong / smart / pretty / rich / famous] enough to make a difference." These are lies that come straight from the father of lies. But they feel true in those hopeless moments, don't they?

It seems like hopelessness is almost an epidemic today, especially among the young. Dr. Jean Twenge talks about how *iGen* (people born between 1995 and 2012 and who came of age when smartphone ownership passed 50%) are significantly delayed by most measures of independence. They aren't motivated. They're much less likely to be working, driving, or even spending time with friends. "18-year-olds now act more like 15-year-olds used to, and 15-year-olds more like 13-year-olds. Childhood now stretches well into high school."[115] All that time on screens is keeping them from growing up. As we saw in previous chapters, screen time is also keeping them depressed and hopeless.

But screens have this effect on all of us regardless of our age. It's just worse for the young since they are more susceptible to being immobilized by addictions[116] and they aren't often forced into the more survival-driven responsibilities of employment or caring for a family.

Yet survival is just the beginning of a positive vision for the future. We long for so much more.

With distraction and hopelessness fighting so hard against our positive vision, we're going to need God's help to see things from his perspective. Thankfully, he is willing and able to give us the clarity and hope we need to lift the fog that clouds our vision.

What's Possible? Vision vs. Purpose

Before we consider what your anticipated future could be, let's first clarify the difference between a *vision* and a *purpose*. They are closely related, and one feeds the other. But the distinction is helpful, and everyone needs both.

I define **vision** as the hopeful anticipation of participating in a certain positive future. In your mind's eye, you look forward to a good potential destination for your life, or—even better—for the good impact you could make in the lives of others. Your picture of the future is big, bright, and compelling: compelling enough to motivate you to make whatever changes that are necessary to make it happen.

Purpose flows from a positive vision. I define **purpose** as a person's specific role in the process of fulfilling their vision. Purpose is the answer to the question, "What am I here for?" but it can't be answered without a vision of what is possible. Pursuing your purpose is the focus of chapter 11, so we'll focus our attention in this chapter to anticipating your positive vision.

We sometimes hear of "vision casting" as something companies do to encourage their businesses to grow, or something political leaders do to inspire their constituents to support them. And leaders who are inspiring enough can cast a vision for a future that calls people to action. Dr. Martin Luther King's "I Have A Dream" speech may be the most famous and compelling vision-casting speech of modern times.

Each of us needs external input to inspire a vision for what is possible in our lives. Most of us see our lives as though we're looking the wrong way through a telescope—as if our lives are small and insignificant. We can't imagine our potential to make a positive impact in the world because we spend too much time focusing on our faults and weaknesses. We have to seek inspiration from the outside to cast a vision for what is *really* possible.

Expect your vision to stretch you, to be bigger than you can imagine doing on your own. You'll know you're on the right track if your vision scares you, because a vision that doesn't depend on God's power and the help of others isn't big enough. We're made for much more than we can do on our own.

I had the honor of working on Dave Ramsey's digital development team for eight years as a senior software developer. Dave is a master of vision casting. He has helped millions of people find financial freedom by showing them *the vision that financial freedom is possible.* He inspires listeners by asking, "What would it be like to have no payments?" He interviews people who have paid off all of their debts and lets them do a *Braveheart*-styled scream of "Freeeeeeedom" to celebrate. These stories show other debt-burdened people what is possible and forms their positive vision. Now filled with hope, they are willing to make countercultural changes: to live on less than they earn, to delay short-term pleasures, to focus on a goal, and to work very hard. Their positive vision motivates them.

When Andy Andrews was homeless and stuck living under a pier in Orange Beach, AL at age 23, it was vision casting that helped him break free. After losing his parents just a couple years before, Andy had lost everything else too, including his perspective. Everything changed when, by God's grace, a mysterious stranger named Jones told Andy that even while living under a pier, he was "on fertile ground." He had potential. And the first thing Jones asked Andy to do was to read inspiring biographies. *Winston Churchill. Will Rogers. George Washington Carver. Joan of Arc. Abraham Lincoln. Viktor Frankl.* Jones told Andy:

> [These books are] adventure stories! Success, failure, romance, intrigue, tragedy, and triumph—and the best part is that every word is true! Remember, young man, experience is not the best teacher. *Other people's* experience is the best teacher. By reading about the lives of great people, you can unlock the secrets to what made them great.[117]

After reading what was possible from the biographies of dozens of inspiring people, Andy distilled seven principles that changed his life. Millions of people around the world have since been impacted by the principles Andy shares through his wonderful stories. Andy's vision was formed after seeing new possibilities he had never considered before.

Legacy

Vision-forming perspective is also found in a more unexpected place: the funeral home. When those close to us pass away, we are inspired by their legacy to either imitate them, or to live differently. Either way, death can have a powerful vision-forming impact on our lives.

In November 2017, I had the sad honor of attending the memorial service of one of my heroes: Bible teacher and best-selling author, Edward Fudge. It was the most joyful, faith-filled, and honoring celebration of a life well lived I've ever seen. His brothers, children, and grandchildren lined up to speak beautiful words of love and gratitude for their brother, dad, and grandpa. But the most powerful words were shared by his wife of 50 years, Sara Faye Fudge, who wrote:

> He was nonjudgmental, humble in spirit, kind in manner and as Jesus described Nathanael, "a man in whom there is no guile." He cherished me for over 50 years, since our first Florida College days, delighted in our two wonderful children, and loved his six precious grandchildren who gave him great joy and hope for the future.[118]

What kind of a vision does it take for a man to cherish his wife for fifty years? Even while facing trials of every kind: powerful opposition, job losses, financial hardships, and tremendous health challenges. And yet, somehow Edward was able to navigate all of these difficulties and more with a steadfast commitment to a higher calling, and as I know he would say, all by the grace of God. What an inspiring legacy.

Speaking of legacy, Jeff Brown, host of the hugely popular "Read to Lead Podcast," recent shared the memory of his 81-year-old dad who had just passed away.[119] The memorial chapel was filled to standing room only with a community of people who were touched by Joe Brown's life. He wasn't a celebrity, nor a YouTube sensation, or a politician. He was just a simple, hardworking man who became renowned in his neighborhood for his kindness, respect, and generosity. Jeff says his dad told the truth to a fault. He was a father figure in the lives of countless neighborhood kids and others who were missing a positive fatherly influence.

I doubt Joe Brown had a smartphone. If he did, he wasn't looking at it when he was sitting on his front porch, waving to the neighbors, always available to share good advice or to lend a hand. And his lifetime of countless and quiet daily kindnesses made such a difference that even his own son didn't realize the impact until the funeral drew in the crowd.

Before dismissing the legacies of Edward Fudge and Joe Brown as impractical relics of a previous age, consider: Did you know that loving your family faithfully for fifty years through every imaginable trial was even possible? Few of us have seen or even heard of such faithfulness. But Edward did it. Did you know that being available to show love to your neighbors could make such an impact? Joe Brown showed us. In a world where few of us know our neighbors (thanks to screens), Joe inspires a different way. Since these men left such a positive legacy, *we all know what is possible, even today.*

Your vision doesn't have to be to change the lives of millions of people like Dave Ramsey or Andy Andrews. It can be as simple (and as challenging) as intentionally fostering a great connection with all of your kids when they are grown up. It can be as important as modeling a real and true relationship with God that inspires your family and friends to know him more.

Anticipating Your Vision

Since becoming a Christian in my senior year of high school, I have felt inspired to make a positive difference in my family and in the world. Yet despite my best intentions, I've often strayed. I've fallen in many ways. But in 2006, I had the strong sense that time was running short and I had better get with it. I had an ever-growing longing to hear God say, "Well done, good and faithful servant" (Matthew 25:21). So, I set out to learn and live the biblical practices that would prepare me for whatever God would ask me to do.

In 2014, I was praying and thinking about the tidal wave of screens smashing into us with their desire-shaping powers. I clearly saw chains forming on those who were becoming trapped in a downward spiral of screen-driven habits and addictions. Each link in their chain was forged by the process we've already seen—they were told what they should want, they acted on that manufactured desire, they felt some short-term pleasure, then they were told what they should want next—an insidious cycle of bondage.

As that vision washed over me, I experienced something spiritually as I have at only a few other times in my life. My heart was broken; I was brought to tears, and the seeds of this book were planted. I'm certain that without a vision from God to stop wasting time and surrender to him completely in 2006, my heart would not have been sensitive in 2014, and I would have missed the chance to share this message with you now.

And here's the message. You are here "for such a time as this" (Esther 4:14). You have been made for something really important and valuable—something you may not even be able to imagine. I couldn't imagine what God was calling me to do; I just had the deep sense that I'd better get ready or I was going to miss it.

Here's some great news: Because of God's unfailing love, and that his mercies are "new every morning" (Lamentations 3:22-23), we are continually given new chances to start again. He has always been in the business of redemption, of helping people start over. New mercies *every morning* means every day is a fresh start. What amazing grace!

And yet, the Bible also shows how our choices matter, and how we can waste our time or become so tangled up with distractions that we can become ineffective and unable to realize our full potential. Esau despised and sold his birthright for a bowl of soup, and his short-sighted desire (along with a manipulative brother) caused him to lose a huge part of his future (Hebrews 12:16). The rich young ruler had a face-to-face mission opportunity from Jesus Christ himself, but turned Jesus down in sadness because he was too attached to his stuff (Mark 10:17-22). Whether we achieve all God made us to do doesn't change how much God loves us, because that's a given. Even so, we must be willing, available, and free from whatever would hold us back.

If you're reading this right now and thinking something like, "I've already fallen too far," or, "I've done too much," or, "I've blown it so there's no hope for me," may I declare to you that those statements consist of more lies from the father of lies. Sure, your bad choices or addictions may have held you back up to now. But that doesn't mean your future is irreparably broken. In fact, God often redeems our failures so we can help others. I've certainly found that to be true. My regrets are now being redeemed to help many people who know that I identify with them. They can see I'm not speaking from some ivory tower of perfection, but from living a life on the ground with those who need what I have to share. Your regrets can be used by God in the same way.

I always tell people that as long as you are breathing, there is hope. God is always waiting, calling people to himself, asking them to turn to him and receive the gift of his love and grace. Jesus is standing at the door knocking (Revelation 3:20), patiently waiting for "whosoever will" to open themselves up to him. Please don't let the enemy use your past to keep you in chains in the present in order to derail your future. Rest in the knowledge of this truth: you are loved, and there is always hope.

But again, the fact that there is always hope doesn't mean we have time to waste. What we do today matters more than any of us realize. It's time to cultivate a vision so important and motivating that we are willing to change, go a different direction, and overcome whatever we must so we don't miss out on what is truly important, what really matters—what, in fact, we've been created to do.

Here's the amazing thing: once you have a clear picture of your positive future, God can use your vision to carry you through any difficulty, distraction, challenge, or fear. Your anticipated vision will powerfully inspire you to overcome whatever is keeping you from the life God has called you to live.

What's Worth It?

Jesus Christ is the best example I know of the power of an anticipated vision. Jesus's clarity enabled him to overcome every distracting temptation. The devil tempted him for forty days in the wilderness by offering Jesus a quick and easy way to gain authority and power in the world. Of course, the promised authority would have been *under* Satan instead of *over* him, but the father of lies didn't mention *that* particular detail in his enticing offer.

Beyond those temptations, Jesus knew he faced a future trial so horrible that we had to invent an English word to describe it: *excruciating.* You can see the "crucified" root in that word. The cross would bring unspeakably intense pain, shame, and worst of all, the sense of being forsaken by his Father (Matthew 27:46). Anticipating his excruciating death, Jesus fell on his face and prayed, "My Father, if it is possible, let this cup pass from Me; yet not as I will, but as You will" (Matthew 26:39).

Facing the real temptation to avoid going to the cross (Hebrews 4:14-16), Jesus somehow didn't give in. He surrendered himself to God's calling, even when it meant torture and death. How was Jesus able to do that? The writer of Hebrews tells us how:

> Fixing our eyes on Jesus, the author and perfecter of faith, **who for the joy set before Him** endured the cross, despising the shame, and has sat down at the right hand of the throne of God (HEBREWS 12:2, emphasis added).

The "joy set before Him" is what enabled Jesus to endure the cross. What was that joy? It was the anticipation of fulfilling his mission, an amazing vision of what was on the other side of the crucifixion. Jesus knew who he was: the promised Messiah (Luke 4:21). He knew what he had come to do, and the benefit of doing it—the redemption of the world (John 3:17). And Jesus trusted his Father's promise to raise him from the dead and give him all authority and power in heaven and on earth (Mark 14:62, Matthew 28:19).

To overcome a world of constant distraction and temptation, to escape the pull of the easy way, and to avoid wasting our lives consuming whatever is popular and enticing, we need to keep something very joyful in front of us, something we can anticipate. Your joyful anticipation may be different from mine. I am driven by the longing to hear God say, "well done." That's something all of us can long for. But you may need something more tangible right now.

If you can't identify a specific and compelling vision for your future, then this is your invitation to take whatever time you need to find it. Unplug—completely—until your vision is clear. Seek God's insight, and the insight of your most trusted mentors. If you don't have a positive environment around you, do what Andy Andrews did and read some inspiring biographies to help you see what's possible. Find a good church and go to lunch with the wisest people there.

Look into the eyes of your kids or the kids around you and think about the legacy you want to leave them. Or, maybe drive across town to a neighborhood suffering under the ravages of drugs and poverty and consider how you might help. Volunteer at the rescue mission, interact with people at the bottom of their addictions, and consider the difference you might make. Above all, get on your knees before the God who loves and calls you, and ask him to open your eyes, to see that "the fields are white for harvest" (John 4:35). Whatever it is, when something intimately connects with you, you will find an inspiring vision.

Absolute Determination

Toward the end of *The Truman Show*, Christof (the director, played masterfully by Ed Harris) is asked whether Truman is essentially imprisoned. Christof answers, "He could leave at any time—if his were more than just a vague ambition. If he was absolutely determined to discover the truth, there's no way we could prevent him." We (spoiler alert) end up seeing Truman's absolute determination pay off.

You and I also need the absolute determination that comes from a clear and positive vision in order to live the lives we are called by God to live. A vision beyond our intentionally addictive screen-filled world cannot include the continual consumption of the same input as everyone else. In fact, our positive vision will result in the opposite: a life of valuable *output* instead of self-focused *input*, a life of important contributions instead of more empty possessions, and a life that produces what the world *really* needs instead of one that consumes what the powerful want us to desire.

We're seeking a better way—a vision of a future where we are free to know the truth and walk in it. A vision beyond being constantly told what to think, or being so distracted we can't think. A vision that is ready, willing, and open to our Creator, who has given us everything we need so we can accomplish what he has prepared for us to do (2 Peter 1:3-4, Ephesians 2:10). For such a time as this.

If you have anticipated your positive vision, your motivating reason, something that is calling you, then you're ready to take the next step. You're ready to join me in learning and applying the biblical practices that have enabled me to walk in more freedom than ever before in my life. You're ready to start moving forward toward your anticipated vision. We'll start in the next chapter with the foundational and most important biblical practice.

CHAPTER 7

[UN]YIELDED

PRACTICE #1: SURRENDER TO CHRIST, THE ANCHOR OF YOUR INTENTIONAL LIFE

An Incomplete Beginning

> The earth is the LORD's, and all it contains,
> The world, and those who dwell in it (PSALM 24:1).[120]

> Then Jesus said to His disciples, "If anyone wishes to come after Me, he must deny himself, and take up his cross and follow Me. For whoever wishes to save his life will lose it; but whoever loses his life for My sake will find it" (MATTHEW 16:24–25).

> "What transforms us is the will to obey Jesus Christ from a life that is one with his resurrected reality day by day, learning obedience through inward transformation."—DALLAS WILLARD [121]

What if the most foundational truth, the reality beneath every other, is so different from what we've heard all our lives that it seems unbelievable? What if that truth is so opposite of what we see on every screen that we can't comprehend it? What if—a terrifying question—we can't see reality for what it is because we've been shaped from birth by false messages?

Before I became a Christian in my senior year of high school, I was an atheist. As a nerdy, science-minded teenager who loved Star Trek, electronics, and programming early computers, I dismissed the idea of God—I considered him to be something make-believe. Religion seemed irrelevant to the new, cool, and more "real" things I was learning in the nascent high-technology world. I admired—maybe even idolized—Mr. Spock, who loved logic and scorned emotions.[122]

More "worldly" interests initially drew me in to the Bible-believing Christian church: girls. I found myself among a group a people who were excited about what the Bible taught, and especially about Jesus Christ, the Son of God who would forgive the sins of anyone who asked him. These people believed the Bible was historical reality, and claimed that God was present and active in their lives. They celebrated with singing and tear-filled testimonies about what Jesus had done for them.

I figured as long as I was attending church, I may as well dig into what was being taught. I wasn't about to pretend anything, since that would be, you know—*illogical.* But if there was a God, and his Son really did come to earth, die on a cross, and rise again from the dead, I wanted to *know.* I wanted to know *him.*

So, I started reading the Bible, books about the Bible, and listening to Christian radio programs. I learned that there were solid reasons to believe in God and Christ. But I wasn't convinced. I felt like I needed a personal experience to tangibly "prove" the truth of the story to my very discerning 17-year-old self.

Finally, on Halloween 1983, a special drama group performed at the church. I don't remember the plot of the show, but I do remember what the speaker said afterwards. The essence of his talk was, "If you're waiting to know whether God is real, that he loves you, and wants to forgive your sins, *you won't know until you actually trust him.* It's just like this chair. I can explain all of the design and engineering that makes this chair work. I can sit on it myself and prove it can hold me. But until you get up, walk over, and sit in the chair yourself, you won't *know* the chair can hold *you.*"

The chair analogy really resonated with me. I got it. I saw that I had been spending time in the theory, but not doing the practical application. I was learning *about* God, but I wasn't actually taking any steps to *know* him.

By God's grace, I accepted the invitation that day, confessing along with the pastor's prayer that I was a sinner, I needed a Savior, and I wanted Jesus, the Son of God, to forgive my sins and put me on the road to eternal life.

It was a profound experience for me. I remember going to bed that night and feeling such a lightness, a hopefulness, and a peace. I felt God's presence and favor. I *knew* God loved me, wanted me to live with him forever, and that he had gone to a lot of trouble to get that message to me. I remember wanting the whole world to feel what I had felt that night.

That was the beginning of a journey with God through Christ that has been wonderful and difficult, blessed and challenging, with many downsides due to my own foolishness, mistakes, fears, baggage, and ongoing sinful ways. Becoming a Christian didn't eliminate all of my problems, and I still fell into some things I now regret.

I think one of the reasons I lacked more freedom from sin and foolishness in my life was that the gospel I received focused almost exclusively on that initial commitment to Christ and the future hope of eternal life. Jesus is the Savior who came to bring those things, for sure, but even more, he is the King of kings and the Lord of all (Revelation 19:16). He has all authority in heaven and on earth (Matthew 28:18). He's not looking for moochers—people who hang out with him for the benefits, but still live however they want. No, he is looking for *disciples*—people who will leave everything and follow him (Luke 5:10-11). He's looking for people willing to *surrender to him completely*.

Aligned to Reality

In his important new book *Salvation by Allegiance Alone*, Matthew Bates argues that our gospel messages should focus more on the *present reality of Jesus as reigning King*. As Bates carefully explains, we are now living between two markers in time: one in the past defined by the death, burial, resurrection, and ascension of Jesus, and the coming future age that will be marked by Jesus's promised return to earth.[123]

As you read this, at this very moment, Jesus is seated "at the right hand of God" (Mark 16:19), as King. The Apostle Paul elaborates:

> . . . which [God] brought about in Christ, when He raised Him from the dead and seated Him at His right hand in the heavenly places, *far above all rule and authority and power and dominion, and every name that is named,* not only in this age but also in the one to come (EPHESIANS 1:19–21, emphasis mine).

Jesus is the King of kings and Lord of lords—right now—and no other so-called authority comes close. That is the present reality, at this very moment. What should be our response? An intellectual agreement to an abstract concept that doesn't impact our daily lives? Definitely not.

Our response should be a fully yielded surrender to our God and King, including our complete, wholehearted, and unconditional *allegiance.*

One of the most important lessons I've learned about surrender comes from the verse I shared at the beginning of this chapter:

> The earth is the LORD's, and all it contains,
> The world, and those who dwell in it (PSALM 24:1).

Ultimately, we own nothing. *Nothing.* We act like things are ours, and talk like it, saying *my* wife, *my* kids, *my* job, *my* money, *my* stuff, *my* time, *my* future. Our mindset shifts profoundly when we recognize that everything belongs to God. The *whole world* is his, including "those who dwell in it." When I no longer see my spouse as mine, but as God's, I treat her with more respect and burden her with fewer expectations. When I treat my kids as if they belong to God, I take my responsibility more seriously while letting go of any desire to build up my ego through their performance.

Living in the truth that God owns everything isn't an add-on for extra-committed people. It's *reality.* When we accept reality and see everything through its lens, surrendering to it, we are aligning ourselves with the truth of how things really are.

Here's another reality we must align with:

> Do you not know that your body is a temple of the Holy
> Spirit who is in you, whom you have from God, and that you
> are not your own? For you have been bought with a price:
> therefore glorify God in your body (1 CORINTHIANS 6:19–20).

Here, Paul is explaining the position we adopt when we become a Christian—when we receive Christ's death on the cross as the sacrifice for our forgiveness, when we declare our allegiance to Christ as Lord of our lives, and we hope in the promise of a wonderful eternal future. Our new position is: God *owns* us. God's Spirit *lives* inside of us, so God owns the deed for our bodies. We're *his* house now, in an even deeper way than Psalm 24:1 conveys. As a result, we have no right to use the "temple" of God in any way in which the owner would not approve. Here's how Os Guinness says it:

> Choice today can always be casual, whereas the covenantal
> vow of faith is costly because we commit ourselves to Jesus
> and mortgage our very selves as we do so. We have chosen,
> and we are committed. We have picked up our crosses,
> and there is no turning back. We are no longer our own.[124]

Again, this isn't a super-spiritual exercise for the ultra-devoted. This is for everyone who wants to align with *reality*. Upon learning this truth, every Christian is expected to do one thing: yield to it. We surrender our whole lives to Christ, since Christ paid for us with his own life.

And this is the truth that answers the terrifying question I posed earlier: *What if we can't see reality for what it is because we've been shaped from birth by false messages?* We've always been told it's *our* life, and we have the *right* to do whatever we *want*. Of course, as we've seen, what we *want* is shaped by those who benefit from bending our desires to their profitable ends.

And here's the surprising irony. When we fully surrender to God, acknowledge that everything belongs to him, and come to depend on him for every breath and heartbeat, something very unexpected happens: we become more free than we've ever been before.

But what does surrender really look like? And is this kind of surrender even possible in today's world?

Practicing Surrender

> Embracing a belief is something you do in your mind. Ac-
> tually surrendering your life is something you can only
> do with your will. And since the only life you have to sur-
> render is the one you're living in this present moment,
> the decision to surrender can only take place right now.[125]

That quote was by Greg Boyd, author of one of the most helpful books I've read on the subject of surrender. It's called *Present Perfect: Finding God in the Now*. The book compiles profound teachings from three men who were known for "practicing the presence of God": Brother Lawrence, Jean-Pierre de Caussade, and Frank Laubach. These three contend that it is possible to be nearly constantly aware of God's Spirit, in an ever-growing, moment-by-moment surrender to his will. Few books I've read have inspired me to make so many highlights and notes. I still have a long way to go on my journey of practicing God's presence, but I'm on the road and am seeing good fruit.

Those who "practice the presence of God" simply seek to be aware of God in nearly every moment. Realizing that the only moment we have to make a decision is this current one, we choose to remember God's reality and reign right now. Many biblical truths teach this; such as, "Be still, and know that I am God" (Psalm 46:10 NIV), "Seek ye first the kingdom of God" (Matthew 6:33 KJV), and, "Do not worry about tomorrow, for tomorrow will care for itself" (Matthew 6:34). Practicing the presence of God embodies Paul's command to "pray without ceasing" (1 Thessalonians 5:17).

> "Stop now and agree with the Lord to live the rest of your
> days in His sacred presence. Then, out of love for Him,
> surrender all other pleasures."—BROTHER LAWRENCE[126]

If you're like me, on first hearing of this idea, you might think it to be very impractical. It might be possible for someone willing to live in a monastery like Brother Lawrence, but we live in a real world with jobs, kids, constant demands, and yes, screens. We can't possibly think of God every moment. We have to think of many other things. And I completely understand: I'm a husband, father, author, speaker, software developer, musician, and many other things. God knows that many moments I miss out on the chance to focus on him. And yet, the more I practice, the more I remain connected with God.

The great thing about the teachings of Lawrence, de Caussade, and Laubach is they are entirely non-condemning. Because we can only surrender in the present moment, our past or future failures (or successes) are not worth focusing on. Boyd says,

> The only relevant question is, Can we remember this truth in this moment, or will our idol-chasing, nonpresent, habitual thoughts take over? We can't answer this question for any future moments. Nor need we condemn or applaud ourselves for how we answered it in past moments. We can only answer this question in this present moment. And now in this one.[127]

It's easy for us to over-complicate the idea of surrender to God in Christ, like there's a bunch of things we have to add to our schedule or sophisticated ideas we need to understand. Boyd challenges that directly:

> For the challenge of living in the Kingdom is not about figuring it out. There's really nothing to figure out! **The challenge, rather, is in submitting to it**. The only information we need to know is that the love of God that was revealed on Calvary surrounds us at every moment and the supreme goal of our life is to surrender to it. The question then is, Will we do this? It's a question that can only be answered with a choice. And this choice can only be made in the present moment.[128]

One of the best things about practicing God's presence is a drop in anxiety. For many people, anxiety is both a motivator for and a result of screen usage. Fear of missing out (FOMO) drives us to check our email or social media accounts. After watching a lot of TV, we feel anxious about what we saw, or what we now think we need. We've already seen the strong correlation between increasing screen time and decreasing mental health.

Boyd says, "Freedom from anxiety is one of the surest evidences you are learning how to abide in Christ moment-by-moment. If we remain surrendered to God, we've already died to everything decay and death could ever threaten to take away."[129] A moment filled with the awareness of God's love and surrender to his will really can't be filled with anxiety. There just isn't room for it.

The important thing is to begin to practice surrender right now. Begin to invite God to participate in whatever you're doing. I find that a quick "thank you, Lord" refocuses my mind toward him. Or, the simple awareness of being held by gravity (thanks to one of Boyd's exercises) can help me remember that "in Him we live and move and have our being" (Acts 17:28 NIV), and I am being loved by God—right now.

> "There remains one single duty. It is to keep one's gaze fixed on the master one has chosen and to be constantly listening so as to understand and hear and immediately obey his will."—JEAN-PIERRE DE CAUSSADE[130]

You can see why I said earlier that surrender to God in Christ is the foundation of any other practice. Without a willing heart—a sincere desire to invite God into every moment—we really can't do anything else of lasting value. Any effort we make to change on our own becomes a fruitless effort of striving that results in failure and frustration. But empowered by God, aware of his presence, love, and power, nothing can keep us from becoming all God wants us to be.

Brother Lawrence said, "We should seek our satisfaction only in satisfying his will."[131] The world constantly offers us satisfaction in so many other things that don't ultimately provide it. But the heart surrendered to God's will brings true satisfaction. Nothing else comes close.

Surrender and Screens

Surrender isn't about becoming passive—it's a cornerstone of an intentional life. You have to purpose to surrender moment-by-moment, because "the lust of the flesh, the lust of the eyes, and the pride of life" is always vigilant and drawing us away from surrender (1 John 2:16). In another irony, surrender can only be maintained by active and constant practice.

How does surrender help to combat the constant pull of screens in our lives? It starts with what we've learned so far: offering our allegiance to God in Christ, and inviting God into the present moment. With open hearts to God and loyalty to King Jesus, we are ready to move forward.

Our use of screens is so often unintentional that we aren't even aware of why we are checking our phone, turning the TV on, or switching from our important computer work to our favorite online distraction. We just do it, habitually. We've already learned about the intentionally habit-forming triggers built into our devices. And in chapter 10, we'll learn how to replace those habits with better ones.

But for now, here are some practical ideas to help you begin to actively practice your surrender:

- Before you check your phone or turn on a show or a game, stop, and surrender that choice to God. Ask for his will in that present moment.
- Delay checking or turning your screen on even for a few minutes. This simple delay can begin to dislodge any addictive triggers and even trigger a quick prayer to God instead.
- Practice the presence of God while viewing anything. Invite him in, ask him what he thinks about what you're seeing, and let him help you limit how long you should be viewing it.
- If you, like me, often find yourself hoping for something when you're about to check—like a certain response to a comment, a long-awaited email, or a certain number of likes—then redirect that hopeful desire for hope in God's love instead. When I feel this competing hope, I often quickly pray, "Lord, my hope is in You alone." When we hope in God, whatever follows becomes less important. If we hope in other things, it can become idolatry, and that never ends well.
- Be willing and open to hear a "no" or "not now" from God. That's part of yielding to his will. God values patience,

self-control, and wholehearted devotion. Expect to spend less time on screens, and more time with him or other people in real time.

- Expect changes to take time. For many of us, changing our relationship with God and screens is a big ship to turn. It will require intentionality. Remember, the creators behind our screen content are the most intentional people around when it comes to keeping your attention. Invest the time to become more intentional about your surrender to God in Christ than the screen manipulators are in their plan to capture you.

What if I Don't Want to?

In a recent radio interview, I was asked this insightful question: "What if I don't want to change?" Maybe you have a similar question after reading all of this stuff about surrender.

If that's you, I'm glad you're still reading. Even if you don't want to change, I want to affirm your self-awareness. Anything you do to learn true things about yourself is positive, and on the path to becoming more intentional. Even the awareness that you don't want to move in a positive direction right now can help you ask more follow-up questions.

There is an obvious cost to surrender. It does mean giving up the ultimate authority of our lives. Surrender is very uncomfortable, and it goes against our natural desires. We want to be in control of ourselves. But the control we think we have over our lives is really an illusion. Dr. Neil Anderson agrees:

> Until we deny ourselves that which was never meant to be ours—the role of being God in our lives—we will never be at peace with ourselves or with God, and we will never be free.[132]

Left to ourselves, the things we want to do are most often inspired by the screens around us. They regularly lead to a vicious cycle of self-indulgent and addicting behaviors. We go from short-term pleasure to pleasure, but ultimately find ourselves dissatisfied. We make little positive progress, and become discouraged when we take a minute to compare where we are to where we really want to go.

The big question is: *why* don't you want to surrender? *Why* don't you want to change? Could it be that your very desires—the motivations inside that make you "want to" or "not want to"—have been shaped by mechanisms designed to keep you doing what you've been doing? Even if it isn't working for you?

The insidious double-bind our media leaders use against us is made of these two messages: "You deserve to do whatever you want," and "Here are the ideas/products/activities [that are most profitable to us] which you *should* want." Further, they constantly repeat the lie that our desires are the truest part of who we are. In reality, we know that our desires change all the time. We are "in the mood" for this or that, or not. A smell or a sound or a commercial excites something inside us, and now we want something we weren't even thinking about a few minutes ago. Our desires can change quickly, given the right input.

Even if you don't want to change right now, but you're (obviously) still reading, I encourage you to pray and ask God to *help you want to change.* Tell him, honestly, that you don't want to, but you *want to want to.* Confess to God that you see the value of surrendering everything to him, but you need help desiring it. Ask God to shape your desires instead of passively giving in to our screen-saturated world. That's a powerful prayer—one he will answer. The change may take time, but Jesus encourages us to keep asking, keep seeking, and keep knocking with the promise that God will give us the good things we need (Matthew 7:7-12).

Covenant Prayer

I was first introduced and led into the path of complete submission to God during my wonderful decade as a member of the Newport (Oregon) Church of the Nazarene. The concept of allegiance to Christ, of being *all-in*, is taught through their focus on God's call to live a holy life. John Wesley, a founder of both the Methodist and Nazarene tribes, well summarized complete surrender in a prayer he introduced to the church in 1755. Here's the modern version as published by the Methodist church. It reflects the high calling of surrender; the challenging but liberating mindset of those of who seek to fully embrace God's loving call.

> I am no longer my own but yours.
> Put me to what you will,
> rank me with whom you will;
> put me to doing,
> put me to suffering;
> let me be employed for you,
> or laid aside for you,
> exalted for you,
> or brought low for you;
> let me be full,
> let me be empty,
> let me have all things,
> let me have nothing:
> I freely and wholeheartedly yield all things
> to your pleasure and disposal.
> And now, glorious and blessed God,
> Father, Son and Holy Spirit,
> you are mine and I am yours. So be it.
> And the covenant now made on earth,
> let it be ratified in heaven.[133]

If you are willing to make the spirit of this prayer a daily practice, then you will lay the foundation for a new life of freedom like you've never known. You'll be able to overcome anything that comes against you, because you are willing to yield everything to your Maker and King. No temptation, whether screen-based or not, can overwhelm someone who yields everything to Almighty God.

And in this submission, you will find peace, freedom, and a new power to live the life you were made to live. Your desires will begin to become what God wants for you, instead of what our culture is constantly trying to pull you into. You'll begin to clearly see the widening gap between the messages of the world and the messages of your loving heavenly Father. And you'll want more of him and less of whatever is served up on some screen.

From this place of surrender, we're on our way to the next biblical practice: repentance from and removal of anything that is holding us back. We'll dive deep into specific things we may need to turn away from and completely eliminate from our lives. A yielded heart, allegiant to Christ, growing in the practice of God's presence, will enable us to willingly set aside anything our Lord shows us. Like a runner with a goal to run a long distance, we will "lay aside every encumbrance" so that we can "run with endurance the race that is set before us" (Hebrews 12:1-2).

CHAPTER 8

[UN]CHANGED

PRACTICE #2: FIND AND REMOVE WHAT ENTANGLES YOU

What Desires?

> "Those whom I love I rebuke and discipline. So be earnest and repent" (REVELATION 3:19 NIV).

> If you keep on doing what you've always done, you will keep on getting what you've always gotten. —AUTHOR UNKNOWN[134]

The big claim of this book is this: our desires are being intentionally shaped by our screens. What we want has been corrupted and is leading us away from the lives we were created to live. When our desires are broken, then our choices will lead us to regrettable and harmful outcomes, and we find out firsthand why God has called those things sinful. But when our focus changes and yields to God and his ways, our desires begin to align with God's desires for us, and the choices that flow from our renewed desires lead to a life of freedom, purpose, and joy.

But there's a problem—a big one. If our desires have been shaped by screens all of our lives, how can we know which of those desires need to change? How can we learn what activities or behaviors should be removed and what can stay? And what happens if we totally blow it and go off the rails—violating what is good and right and true—even when we know better?

King of Repentance

The exciting and sometimes tragic story of King David's life helps to answer these questions. Promoted from lowly shepherd boy to king of God's chosen people, David is remembered as a handsome warrior, a skilled musician, a beloved leader, a dear friend, and most significantly, a man after God's own heart (1 Samuel 13:14; Acts 13:22). But David is also known for his terribly sinful failures.

Nearly everyone knows the story of David and Bathsheba from 2 Samuel 11. David sees the beautiful woman bathing, commits adultery with her, and after hearing she's pregnant, he tries several schemes to make it look like the coming child is her husband Uriah's. But Uriah is too devoted to the king to play along, so David has him killed and marries Bathsheba himself. How can such a blatant adulterer and murderer be considered a man after God's own heart, especially by the Apostle Paul?

Here's how. When confronted with the true, dark, and evil reality of his choices, David immediately confessed. He didn't try to hide it or explain it away. He didn't start a cover-up story or use his vast wealth to hire high-octane lawyers or pay people off. He simply and humbly repented.

In 2 Samuel 12, we read that God sent the prophet Nathan to confront David. After David heard the charges, he responded with the simple confession, "I have sinned against the LORD." Immediately, Nathan shared God's gracious response, "The LORD also has taken away your sin; you shall not die." There were still to be serious consequences for David's sins, but his heart immediately returned to God when he was confronted.

Up until that time, David lived in a fog created by his sinful desires. He had lost his former focus and devotion to God and his ways, and was just doing what felt good to him. Following that path to its inevitable conclusion, he became a murdering adulterer. But God, in his never-ending love, with new mercies every morning (Lamentations 3:22-23), graciously confronts David and offers him the opportunity to confess and repent from his sin.

While several psalms reveal David's repentant heart, Psalm 51 records his confession and plea to God following his sin with Bathsheba.

> Wash me thoroughly from my iniquity
> And cleanse me from my sin.
> For I know my transgressions,
> And my sin is ever before me (PSALM 51:2–3).

Then after pouring out his heart to God, David asks for restoration.

> Create in me a clean heart, O God,
> And renew a steadfast spirit within me.
> Do not cast me away from Your presence
> And do not take Your Holy Spirit from me.
> Restore to me the joy of Your salvation
> And sustain me with a willing spirit (PSALM 51:10–12).

While David's life from that point on was a mess, he continued to trust God. His trust in God was memorialized by David and Bathsheba's second child—Solomon, the next king of Israel—as he dedicated the new temple he built:

> [Solomon] said, "O LORD, the God of Israel, there is no god like You in heaven or on earth, keeping covenant and showing lovingkindness to Your servants who walk before You with all their heart; who has kept with Your servant David, my father, that which You have promised him; indeed You have spoken with Your mouth and have fulfilled it with Your hand, as it is this day" (2 CHRONICLES 6:14–15).

It seems that David's walk before God with all his heart included the willingness to be corrected when he fell. He completely lost his way, but when confronted, he immediately returned. God didn't expect perfection of David; just a faithful willingness to follow and to admit when he went wrong. This same David wrote Psalm 23, proclaiming the comfort of God's "rod and staff"—the tools of the shepherd for helping wayward sheep stay on the right path.

Repentance, or turning away from sin, was a significant part of Solomon's prayer of dedication for the temple. Listen to these still-relevant words Solomon prayed on behalf of his people.

> "When they sin against You (for there is no man who does not sin) and You are angry with them and deliver them to an enemy, so that they take them away captive to a land far off or near, if they take thought in the land where they are taken captive, and repent and make supplication to You in the land of their captivity, saying, 'We have sinned, we have committed iniquity and have acted wickedly'; if they return to You with all their heart and with all their soul in the land of their captivity, where they have been taken captive, and pray toward their land which You have given to their fathers and the city which You have chosen, and toward the house which I have built for Your name, then hear from heaven, from Your dwelling place, their prayer and supplications, and maintain their cause and forgive Your people who have sinned against You" (2 CHRONICLES 6:36–39).

Several important thoughts stand out here. God always makes provision for the forgiveness of sin, knowing that everyone gets off track, and will need a way back so we can "return with all our heart and soul." The way we are to find our way back is to "repent and plead with [God]" (NIV). In Solomon's case, because the presence of God was focused on the new temple, they were to pray "toward the house which I have built for Your name." Following the sacrificial death and resurrection of Christ, the physical direction of our prayers isn't important anymore, but the idea is the same: aim your life at God's presence. For me, that physical direction is *down*, on my knees.

There are at least four steps in the process of repentance—a process that involves deliberate turning away from whatever is holding us back and turning to God, to follow him in yielded surrender with all our hearts.

Repentance begins with **knowledge** of the problem. We can't stop doing something we don't know is wrong. In David's case, the prophet Nathan brought the message and helped David see what he had done and understand that God was condemning David's sin. This is a counter-cultural thing to do today. One popular cultural message is "don't judge," meaning it's never right to offer a correction to anyone. We can't label anything as "wrong" because that is critical and judgmental. As a result, a lot of people are doing things that are damaging to themselves or others, and nobody tells them. But God says, "those whom I love, I reprove and discipline" (Revelation 3:19). It's loving to help people know what they need to change, because we can't change unless we *know* what needs to change.

Next, repentance requires **openness**, or a willingness to be corrected. This comes from the previous chapter's practice—cultivating a heart of surrender to God through Christ, the King of our lives. Christ followers must always remain open to being guided by God to better paths, which includes being told that something we are doing needs to change.

Following knowledge of the problem and openness to consider it, we must follow with our **agreement**. This is the time when we evaluate what we've heard, compare it to the Bible, and seek the advice of trusted mentors to make sure we're hearing correctly. Once verified, we must agree that the issue at hand really does apply to us.

Finally, we must act on what we've learned by actually making the needed **change**. To repent is to change our minds, and therefore, change our direction. With our newfound knowledge, openness, and agreement about the issue, we must take the action to turn away. And in turning *away*, we turn *toward* God, following Christ as he leads us on good and right paths.

It's important to remember that God is active throughout this entire process. He sent Jesus Christ to die on the cross for our sins because of his great love and his desire that we turn away from every self-destructive thing we do (John 3:16). He sent the Holy Spirit after Jesus's resurrection and ascension so he could convict the world of things that needed to change (John 16:7-11). And he is always "faithful and righteous to forgive us our sins and to cleanse us from all unrighteousness" (1 John 1:9).

What Needs to Change?

But back to the question from the beginning of this chapter: how can we gain the *knowledge* of what we need to change? If Nathan the prophet doesn't show up at our dinner table, how can we learn whether there are things we are doing that are taking us off track, away from God's best for us? Especially since we often either find it hard to see our own faults, or we can be overly critical of ourselves. Both extremes are unproductive, so we need to find a helpful and trustworthy outside source to help us see ourselves and our actions correctly.

The Bible is the best place to learn what we need to change. God has graciously preserved anointed words for thousands of years. These unchanging standards of goodness and truth are still relevant and applicable to all of us, even in our confused, distracted, and noisy era.

The Ten Commandments of Exodus 20 are a great baseline. Read them, and then start to reflect on them with an open heart. For example, what about the second command—*no idols.* Is there anything in your life, especially on a screen, that has become an idol? Something that might make an observer from another planet think you were worshipping it? Or that tenth command—*do not covet*—does anything you're doing on a screen make you feel envious or jealous? Comparison traps lurk all over social media.

Jesus re-affirms the Big Ten in the Sermon on the Mount of Matthew 5-7, and increases the intensity of a couple of them. For Jesus, refraining from murder is not enough; instead, we need to stay away from the anger that leads us to feel hateful (Matthew 5:21-26). Likewise, the act of adultery isn't the line Jesus wants us to avoid; we must keep the *desire* for adultery out of our hearts (Matthew 5:27-30). Certainly, much screen-based content is designed to entice our hearts away from Jesus's standard. As you open yourself to these commands, ask God to give you a soft heart and a tender conscience so you'll be able to see where you need to course-correct.

For the Scriptures to be most effective, it is vital to regularly attend a church where the Bible is preached clearly and accurately. God can use pastors and teachers to help us see what we can't on our own. Also, small groups of believers focused on growing disciples of Christ are critical. I find a close-knit group of trusted friends where intentionally *real* conversations happen to be one of the best ways I learn what needs to change. If you don't have a church and a small group of close Christian believers in your life, I encourage you to take tangible steps toward them.

You might not find yourself violating Ten Commandments or even Sermon on the Mount standards much these days. As you reflect on your life, you may be living as a maturing disciple of Christ who isn't frequently tempted by those things. That's a great place to be, but it doesn't necessarily mean there's nothing new for you to turn away from.

Consider 1 Corinthians 6:12, where Paul says, "All things are lawful for me, but not all things are profitable. All things are lawful for me, but I will not be mastered by anything."

Paul shows how there can be areas of our lives that aren't sinful per-se, but they may not be good for us. In fact, there may be certain things that are fine for other people, but not for you. Those are things that are holding you back. Those things may not dominate or master others, but in your life, they are like a chain that wraps around your spirit and drags you down.

"Therefore be careful how you walk, not as unwise men but as wise, making the most of your time, because the days are evil" (Ephesians 5:15-16). The King James version says, "redeeming the time, because the days are evil." In a day when we are surrounded by a thousand time-wasting distractions—things that aren't sinful in and of themselves but have the effect of keeping us from our God-given purpose—we have to be extra "wise" to "make the most of our time."

As you look back at your use of time, maybe recalling the evaluation you did in chapter 5 with a newly opened of heart toward God, ask yourself some hard questions. Here are some examples:

- Are you making real progress toward your vision, or are you just making progress on social media?
- Do you have time with God in prayer and Bible reading every day, or do you just have time on Netflix?
- Are you stressed financially with a low amount of savings, but your video game scores are high?

- Are you angry or afraid about the state of the world, but you turn on Fox News or CNN every morning?
- Do you often say there's not enough time to get everything done, while you have many hours a day on a screen?

Dave Ramsey often says, "I've never met a millionaire who knows who was thrown off the island." He means that people who make real progress in their lives don't get caught up in "reality" TV or any other time-draining activity. They are focused on their goals and they don't let anything trivial get in their way.

If you're letting too much precious time profit screen content creators who are more intentional about your time than you are, then I encourage you to *redeem your time*. Repent of wasting the gift of the time you've been given in your one life, which is "just a vapor that appears for a little while and then vanishes away" (James 4:14).

What Needs to Go?

> Therefore, since we have so great a cloud of witnesses surrounding us, let us also lay aside every encumbrance and the sin which so easily entangles us, and let us run with endurance the race that is set before us (HEBREWS 12:1).

As we grow in a life of freedom through surrender to God in Christ and invite him to identify things we need to stop doing, we also will find things we need to completely remove from our lives. It won't be enough to just do them a little less, or try a little harder to avoid them once in a while. If we're going to break free, once and for all, some things are just going to have to go.

Immediately when I say this, I hear objections like, "What? I can't unplug from everything!" Believe me, I get it, and I understand how hard it can be to think of removing certain things from our lives. However, if hearing "some things are going to have to go" results in immediate push-back, something may not be as surrendered as it should be.

I'm not advocating an Amish existence, or removal of every screen. On the other hand, I'm not suggesting "balance" in our use of technology, or anything else. The problem with the idea of "balance" is that everyone thinks they are balanced. Each of us is the most moderate person we know, right? We don't do this or that as much as some other people we know, so we must be balanced, right? Striving for balance lets us off the hook and keeps us "encumbered" and "entangled."

In *The Great Divorce*, C.S. Lewis depicts a man with a beloved temptation personified in the form of a red lizard who is always clasped around him and constantly whispers in his ear. An angel who wants to help the man break free calmly tells him that the *lizard must die*. However, the lizard doesn't want to die, and the man is very reluctant to let him be killed as well. The man comes up with excuse after excuse to delay the process. The angel calmly continues to insist that the *lizard must die*, and die *now*. The process will hurt the man, but not kill him, the angel promises. All the angel needs is the man's willing permission. Finally, the man agrees, the lizard is killed, and the result is a glorious new life of freedom.

Dr. Joshua Straub, author of *Safe House*, says, "whatever you cannot fast from, owns you." If there is something in your life that you hope God will not ask you to remove, then that thing may be an idol in your life, something that owns you, instead of being owned by you. If it's your smartphone, Dr. Jean Twenge replies, "Let your phone be a tool you use – not a tool that uses you."[135]

A posture of surrender, remembering that God owns everything and we belong to him, really helps to make removing entanglements easier. I am motivated by 2 Timothy 2:4 as well, which says, "No soldier in active service entangles himself in the affairs of everyday life, so that he may please the one who enlisted him as a soldier." If I'm like an honorable soldier, one who is focused on the mission instead of what everyone else is watching or liking, then I'm willing to lay aside what everyone else is doing in order to succeed in my mission.

What would make your home a sanctuary that allows you to be free to seek and follow God where he wants to lead you? To become the kind of parent or spouse or employee or volunteer that he needs you to be? Is it a subscription? A connection? A social media account or three? A mobile device or three? A game console or three?

Is it a TV in your bedroom, or a device you use like a TV? If you're married, I think a TV in your bedroom is incredibly damaging to your relationship. There's literally no benefit. If the television is on (or even just present), you're adding distraction, stress, and anxiety into what should be your sanctuary, while also blocking connection and intimacy. You're not available for a quiet talk, a snuggle, making love, or even just a good night's sleep. Most importantly, whether you're married or not, you're inviting the most carefully crafted content—*specifically designed to manipulate you*—into your mind at the precise time your defenses are down and you're most vulnerable. You're tired, and as you fall asleep, your subconscious is more open, so you'll dream of the things they want you to want, and become more entangled. I try not to be too proscriptive, because everyone has their own issues. But I am confident that if you have a TV or some other video device in your bedroom (including your phone), it needs to go. If you are reluctant, just try it for a month (or three) and see what happens. If you protest that your phone is your alarm clock, simply go to a local store and buy a real alarm clock. Again, try it and see what happens.

What about certain content? The challenging thing is that our culture has so normalized sexualized and violent visuals that we might not even notice them pulling us off track. However, verses like these in Ephesians 5 provide warnings we need to consider:

> For you were formerly darkness, but now you are Light in the Lord; walk as children of Light (for the fruit of the Light consists in all goodness and righteousness and truth), trying to learn what is pleasing to the Lord. Do not participate in the unfruitful deeds of darkness, but instead even expose them; for it is disgraceful even to speak of the things which are done by them in secret (EPHESIANS 5:8–12).

When Paul says, "do not participate in unfruitful deeds of darkness," remember—watching is participating. By consuming, you're voting for that content. You're paying for it, either directly or by watching ads. By watching, you're thanking the industry for paying those actors to entertain you in those ways. Watching feels passive, but it's not. It just feels that way because it is intentionally designed to be tempting and easy to consume.

Tim Challies posted a helpful blog titled "Are you Godly enough to watch smut?"[136] He argues that among many Christians, watching nudity and sexuality is almost considered virtuous. It's like the more spiritual we are, the more immorality should be able to watch without being affected by it. He says, "Today it is considered a sign of spiritual maturity to watch scenes of nudity and sexuality and a sign of spiritual weakness to refrain. [. . .] It is considered absurd that perhaps, just perhaps, this is the sign of a hardened rather than a tender conscience." If this is your perspective, I encourage you to seek, with a yielded heart, to understand what Paul is calling us to in Ephesians 5. Could it be that our media is leading Christians away from the purity of thought and action that God desires for us? As a Christian, would you really expect to be able to watch and enjoy what non-Christians revel in? Shouldn't there be a difference?

Years ago, we removed cable and broadcast TV from our lives. We still don't have Netflix. We are very judicious about the movies we bring into our home, occasionally using services like VidAngel to filter content. Some movies require so much filtering they aren't worth watching in the first place. As we'll see in the next chapter, the input we receive shapes our thinking and becomes our output. We can't help it. You may need to remove your TV services too, and significantly filter what you do allow into the sanctuary of your home.

What about your smartphone? Here's a mind-blowing thought: some people shouldn't have one. The smartphone is like a mental allergy to them that sickens their thinking. To be healthy and free, they're going to need to move to a flip phone instead. There is absolutely no shame in that. Nobody needs a smartphone. Really. Let me say that again: *Nobody needs a smartphone.* Maybe that's the lizard in your life that needs to die. If you are one of the many people who just can't have a smartphone, that doesn't mean you're weak; in fact, it means exactly the opposite. You will show tremendous strength and character if you go against culture and remove it from your life.

And you know what else? Your kids *definitely* don't need a smartphone. There is no upside to them—none. If you want to know why, read Melanie Hempe's list of "7 Reasons Kids Don't Need a Smartphone."[137] She quotes Melinda Gates, who says, "For adolescents who don't yet have the emotional tools to navigate life's complications and confusions, [smartphones] can exacerbate the difficulties of growing up: learning how to be kind, coping with feelings of exclusion, taking advantage of freedom while exercising self-control."[138] If you've followed cultural norms and given your children smartphones, I encourage you to read more on Hempe's site, and take steps to love your kids enough to keep them from the addicting damage of screens.

In addition, you may need to evaluate and possibly remove or significantly limit devices like computers or tablets. (If you haven't seen the movie *Fireproof*, watch it sometime to see the scene where the main character removes his computer—forcefully.) For those of us who use computers for work, we may need to apply aggressive filters instead. There are several great companies that provide filtering for every device. Covenant Eyes,[139] Forcefield,[140] and Circle[141] are just a few of the options available. They aren't just for kids; they are for anyone who wants to remove any modern "encumbrance" in the most decisive and effective way possible.

I know that removing these devices sounds pretty extreme. And it is. If you have a family, it will take some careful, prayerful, and vision-filled talks to make any changes you feel God leading you to make. If you just show up one day and get rid of a bunch of screens, you're going to have a mutiny on your hands. That's why it's so important to start with vision, then move toward surrender, and then invite your family along for a positive journey. Everyone needs to at least begin to agree that they want their desires to be shaped by God through Christ, and not by intentionally manipulative screens. Kids may especially resist, so take slow, careful steps. But in the end, you're the parent, and you know what is best. For more helpful reasons and ideas, read articles by Dr. Meg Meeker. I'll share a couple in the footnotes.[142]

More Than You Can Do Alone

Turning away from whatever is holding us back is challenging for everyone. But if, after you've prayed, studied, pursued these things in a good church and small group, and made some decisions, you still find yourself unable to break free, you may have an addiction that will need more focused attention. If that's you, I'm proud of you for realizing your need for help. Not one of us can become all God wants us to be without the help of others.

There are some outstanding Christian addiction recovery groups, and they aren't just for physical substance addictions. I have found Celebrate Recovery (CR) to be an especially gracious organization. CR is a 12-step program like AA, but it is completely focused on a specific "higher power," Jesus Christ. CR also seems more positive in its mindset, in my (admittedly limited) experience. In AA, it seems like a person's addiction can become their identity, as in, "Hi, I'm ____, and I'm an alcoholic." In CR, participants are encouraged to identify as "a grateful follower of Jesus Christ who has struggled with . . ." That difference is profound.

There are CR meetings all over the country, moderated by gracious and kind people who have overcome all kind of hurts, habits, and hang-ups by God's grace. CR actively helps people who struggle with behavioral addictions like video gaming, gambling, compulsive social media, or other intentionally addictive technologies. If you try it, you may be surprised when you meet other people who are struggling with the same addictions as you may be.

If you're thinking to yourself, "I should probably think about doing that someday," I encourage you to do it now. Go to CR's website at http://celebraterecovery.com and find a group. Show up, with all the openness you can muster. See what God will do in your life. Isn't it time to find the freedom from compulsive behaviors or deep-seated pain you've always wanted? If not now, when?

If the CR idea just can't work for you right now because you are just unable to bring yourself to a group situation, then your addiction may require professional one-on-one counseling. Find a Christian counselor, hopefully one who is referred to you by your pastor or someone else you trust, who will help you with biblically-based addiction recovery techniques. God uses professionals of every kind, in addition to the power of his Word and his Spirit, to enable us to become all he has called us to be. Do whatever you need to do to overcome whatever you need to overcome.

Light and Free

I'm not sure why our current age seems so resistant to hearing that we may need to make a change. How can we grow without changing? Nobody is born knowing everything, and we all fail in many ways. In fact, "all have sinned and fall short of the glory of God" (Romans 3:23). That statement is a great equalizer and a humility-builder. Everyone has blown it—God knows I have blown it big time. But why would we want to keep doing the very things that are destroying us?

In an era where much that was formerly wrong is now celebrated, where addictive short-term pleasure fuels much of the U.S. economy, it's culturally sacrilegious to suggest that someone is doing something less than optimal, or even wrong, and they need to change. But I'm grateful that you are still with me and are open to the idea that, like me, you may have things you need to stop doing—course corrections you need to make—and maybe even have some things that need to be completely removed from your life. Even if those changes are completely weird, counter-cultural, or something nobody else you know would do, I am proud of you and know you will be very glad you have taken these positive steps.

In my experience, there is a lightness, a freedom, and a joy that comes from turning away from something that has kept me from God's best. Even so, repentance and removal aren't one-and-done events. Proverbs 24:16 says, "a righteous man falls seven times, and rises again." Even if we are pulled back into something we turned away from, we don't give up. We surrender to God again; repent again; and further, we evaluate what happened and take steps to remove whatever must be eliminated to make it much less likely that we'll fall again. And we always remember that as long as we're alive, God's gracious mercies are new every morning (Lamentations 3:23). He loves to forgive and restore us whenever we ask.

With lives formed by a practice of ongoing, yielded surrender, plus this practice of turning away from and removing anything that God asks us to change, we are ready to go even deeper. I'm excited about the next chapter because we get to focus on adopting a practice of re-newing our minds. Every decision we've made, for good or bad, has started in our thoughts. And our screens do everything they can to encourage us to think like the content producers want us to think. But our Creator's way of thinking is best for us, and he has given us everything we need to be able to think like he does, even in a world flooded with opposing messages. May he transform us as we continue our journey together.

CHAPTER 9

[UN]TRANSFORMED

PRACTICE #3: RENEW YOUR MIND WITH WHAT'S REAL AND TRUE

Using Moses Against You

> Do not conform to the pattern of this world, but be transformed by the renewing of your mind. Then you will be able to test and approve what God's will is—his good, pleasing and perfect will (ROMANS 12:2 NIV).

> "Our useless thoughts spoil everything. They are where mischief begins. We ought to reject such thoughts as soon as we perceive their impertinence to the matter at hand. We ought to reject them and return to our communion with God." —BROTHER LAWRENCE[143]

There's never been a time when people were more constantly bombarded with input than in the current age of the smartphone. At nearly every moment of the day or night, some media or another is fighting to embed its message deep into our brains. Shocking visuals and sounds all wrestle for our attention; enticing animated GIFs distract us; and more scandalous social media stories draw us into doing whatever they can do to get us to notice them.

We stand in front of screens in restaurants, stores, lobbies, and airports; we set up screens in every room of our homes and even in our cars. If not screens, then music or talk radio are implanting their ideas. We spend more time than ever in the bathroom with our phones, and there are even waterproof speakers and screen covers for our showers, lest we ever have a moment of silence to experience a thought of our own. Each of these media delivery devices, as you know, are intentionally designed by those who spend billions of dollars and millions of hours to inject their thoughts into our heads. With constant exposure to media, we end up approving of and cheering for whatever idea or cause or product or style or even way of looking at ourselves and the world they choose for us.

Media leaders from Silicon Valley to Madison Avenue, inspired by Bernays's propaganda techniques, know what the ancient Israelites were taught over 3,500 years ago: Whatever thoughts fill your days will certainly shape who you become. That's why God, through Moses, taught the newly freed slaves a way of mind-shaping that most of us have ignored, but one media leaders use against us as though they were our priests:

> These words, which I am commanding you today, shall be on your heart. You shall teach them diligently to your [children] and shall talk of them when you sit in your house and when you walk by the way and when you lie down and when you rise up. You shall bind them as a sign on your hand and they shall be as frontals on your forehead. You shall write them on the doorposts of your house and on your gates (DEUTERONOMY 6:6–9).

Isn't this exactly what our culture does (though with different content than God had in mind)? What do most people do when they sit at home, or when they drive around? Before they go to sleep and as soon as they wake up? What do they wear on their hands or keep in front of their faces? What is hanging on our walls? Can you see the uncomfortable parallels?

There isn't a more effective way to change a nation, or a world. Every day—morning until night, eating, sleeping, traveling, at bus stops, train stations, hanging out with friends, working—implant a message on everyone's heart. And what do our screens want us to have on our hearts? The latest presidential Tweet. *The Bachelor.* Kanye. Beyoncé. The latest scores. What she looks like now. How many followers or likes you have. Or a video game-powered retreat from all that noise into a different world. Either way, if you're not intentionally choosing and filtering and ordering what you bring into your mind, your screens will be happy to tell you what to think and how to feel and what to want—all day, every day of your life.

Because the people who create the content on your screens know the truth we often forget: *You become what you think about.*

The Bible spends a lot of time focusing on what is in our *heart*—the most inward part of who we are. Deuteronomy 6:6 starts with, "These words, which I am commanding you today, shall be on your *heart.*" When Jesus was confronting the appearance-obsessed Pharisees, he redirected them to the truth, "For out of the *heart* come evil thoughts, murders, adulteries, fornications, thefts, false witness, slanders." (Matthew 15:19). Jesus may have had the famous proverb in mind, "Guard your *heart* above all else, for it determines the course of your life" (Proverbs 4:23 NLT).

Now you can see why there is such a competition to fill your mind with constant and tantalizing input. The creators know if they can be top of mind—if you're singing along to their song, cheering for their brand, or staring at their app—then they will ultimately direct the course of your life.

But their course leads only to emptiness and regret. When we spend too much time on our screens, we become used up, exploited, drained, and worn-out data serfs, lacking sleep and energy, filled with propaganda-inspired anxieties and fears, compelled by deceptions to yearn for the "next big thing." All further reinforced by the imperative to keep up with everyone else, which is easy since we're all being programmed with the same messages.

So what can we do?

By the grace of God we can, with a yielded heart and a willingness to be changed, become transformed by the renewing of our minds

(Romans 12:2). We can literally become a new person—driven by completely different motives and values than the world around us—by becoming intentional with our thoughts. This works because it aligns with the way God made us. We are shaped by the input we receive. What fills our mind fuels our decisions and becomes our future.

Transformed into What?

Like the miraculous metamorphosis we see when a caterpillar becomes a butterfly,[144] God wants us to become like him, as we see most perfectly modeled in Jesus Christ. He wants us to be known by the fruit of his Spirit, "love, joy, peace, patience, kindness, goodness, faithfulness, gentleness, self-control" (Galatians 5:22-23a). When we become a person who is characterized primarily by these traits, we'll be almost unrecognizable from who we were before.

A screen-saturated mind motivates most of us toward a relentless self-focus. When we are constantly being asked what we want, what we like, enticed to short-term pleasure and "fun" as defined by culture, the fruit ends up being the exact opposite of the godly characteristics described in Galatians 5. Just think of what fills most social media. Would any of the nine fruits of the Spirit describe it? Or is it more filled with the opposite—perhaps what could be called the Fruit of the Screen: selfishness,[145] regret, anxiety, impatience, meanness, evil, disloyalty, harshness, and self-indulgence?

The most famous mind-renewal verse in the Bible is Romans 12:2. It radiates with depth and richness of meaning—enough to fill a book by itself. The challenge: don't be *conformed*, but be *transformed*. "Conformed" is such a great way of describing us when our lives are immersed in screens. It's why I've being saying our desires are *shaped*, like when metal is melted down and then poured into a mold to *form* it into the shape desired by the metalworker. The metal *conforms* to the shape of the mold, just like we are *conformed* by the spirit of our age when we allow them to Deuteronomy-Six us with their messages. By renewing our minds with God's truth, we can be literally reshaped into the mold God designed for us.

And, there's something even more important in this verse that I missed for many years. The reason we are to be transformed is so we "will be able to test and approve what God's will is—his good, pleasing, and perfect will (NIV)."[146] The Greek word rendered "test and approve" here is δοκιμάζειν (dokimazein),[147] which appropriately comes from metalworking. It means to test and verify that a metal is genuine, such as when a goldsmith wants to validate the purity of gold before making a ring. After the metal is verified, the goldsmith *approves* of it for its designated use, because it is the real thing.

This is God's ultimate goal: that we would personally, internally, and completely approve of his good, pleasing, and perfect will. When we hear God's will, he wants us to genuinely love it, cheer for it, and say "Yes, God, I *love* your ideas!" He wants to make us into the kind of people who are *like him* because we have been transformed to love him and his ways.

Approving what God loves involves a process of maturation much like the process of growing from a child into a wise adult. God doesn't want our motives to be like a two-year-old who only stays in the yard because he will get in trouble, or the sixteen-year-old who will only do her homework so she can go to her friend's party. He wants us to say, "Yes, Father!" whenever we recognize his goodness, wisdom, and loving guidance. God hopes we will *want* to follow him, not because he forces us, but because we are genuinely attracted to his kind invitation.

This is what Psalm 37:4 is getting at when it says, "Delight yourself in the LORD; And He will give you the desires of your heart." God wants us to be excited about him and what he is up to. He wants us to find him more delightful than anything else this world has to offer. When our thinking is transformed, then the desires of our hearts are changed into what he desires, and we become his enthusiastic advocates.

When Jesus taught us to pray, "Your kingdom come. Your will be done, on earth as it is in heaven" (Matthew 6:10), he wanted us to *mean* it. God wants us to *want* his kingdom to come, to long for his will to be done on earth as in heaven. This is a mind-transforming prayer, which is why so many of us pray it every day. I pray the Lord's prayer first thing every morning. I'm aware of the risk of this prayer becoming a mindless ritual, so to fight this temptation, I surrender to God, check my motives, and from my heart, really *pray*, asking for God's kingdom and will to take over everything.

How do we become the kind of people who really want what God wants, who delight in him and his ways? We adopt both sides of this mind-renewing practice. On one side, we relentlessly filter the input we receive so we are not deceived and pulled away from God's truth. On the other, we allow God to transform us by filling our minds with what he knows to be real and true.

Limited Capacity

What if every thought you had was positive, productive, wise, and important? What if you had a never-ending flow of good ideas, creative solutions, and insightful things to say? What if every decision you made was the best one under the circumstances, and you had no regrets? Sounds good, right? If anything close to this is possible, where would the thoughts behind such wise decisions come from?

They would come from a mind completely filled with what is true, honorable, right, pure, lovely, and good (Philippians 4:8). This is why it's so vital to carefully decide what you will store in your mind. Your life tomorrow depends on your thinking today.

As you've probably experienced, nobody has an endless mental capacity. Our minds are truly amazing, but they are limited.

The iconic master detective Sherlock Holmes knew this well. As depicted by Sir Arthur Conan Doyle, Holmes was always the most observant and insightful person in the room. However, Watson was shocked to learn that his brilliant friend didn't have a third grader's knowledge of the solar system. Holmes shared his insightful reason for this apparent lack of knowledge:

> I consider that a man's brain originally is like a little empty attic, and you have to stock it with furniture as you choose. [. . .] **Now the skillful workman is very careful indeed as to what he takes into his brain-attic. He will have nothing but the tools which may help him in doing his work, but of these he has a large assortment, and all**

in the most perfect order. It is a mistake to think that that little room has elastic walls and can distend to any extent. Depend upon it, there comes a time when for every addition of knowledge you forget something that you knew before. It is of the highest importance, therefore, not to have useless facts elbowing out the useful ones.[148]

Doyle's fictional detective has important wisdom for all of us. Why do we so carelessly allow any random input to fill our minds? Is it any wonder we feel overwhelmed or anxious and unable to make the progress we want to make on the important things we'd love to have done by now, when our thoughts are so crowded by a constant barrage of media?

The great news is that we can always clean our brain-attic and make room for what is good. We *can* be transformed by renewing our minds. No matter what we've filled our minds with in the past, we can start now, allowing God's truth to shape us into the kind of people who think and act like he would want us to. As Zig Ziglar says,

> You are what you are and where you are because of what has gone into your mind. You can change what you are and where you are by changing what goes into your mind.[149]

If we become intentional about what we allow into our minds, we will find ourselves filled with the thoughts that will help us become all we're made to be. Let's consider some strategies to move us in this direction.

Renewing Strategies

I experienced an important mental paradigm shift while reading the work of Charles G. Finney many years ago. The great nineteenth-century evangelist taught that we can think of our minds as having three functional areas: the will (choices), the intellect (thoughts), and the sensibilities (feelings). Finney confirmed what we all know when we are quiet and unplugged: Our will is in the driver's seat of the other two functions. With our God-given power to choose, we can decide what we think about. And if we focus on a certain line of thought long enough, our feelings will follow by what Finney calls a "law of necessity," or a law of nature.

This paradigm is exactly opposite of what we learn from most screens. We're taught that our feelings are in the driver's seat. Our popular culture says that whatever we *feel* is the truest part of who we are, so we should behave in ways that line up with how we are feeling. And yet, we also know that our feelings are the most volatile, unstable part of who we are. Messages that manipulate us do so by trying to change how we feel. Those manipulations can only work when we choose to let our feelings sit on our will's lap in the driver's seat of our mind.

Ultimately, our choices and decisions are made by our will. The reason for any choice may be that we listened to our feelings, or we may have used our intellect to listen to true and wise ideas. But either way, our will directs our thoughts; from there, our feelings must eventually follow.

Another important part of the will > thoughts > feelings paradigm is that *we are not our thoughts.* Instead, we are the person who is able to decide what to think about. I used to be very anxious about disturbing, scary, or even outright evil thoughts that sometimes arise in my mind. What kind of person was I to think such things? What could they mean?

Here's the life-changing truth: If you are thinking about what you're thinking about, then *you* are evaluating your thoughts. You're deciding what to think about each idea that arises in your mind. Notice the distinction: there's *you,* and then, separately, there is what you're thinking about.

You get to decide what to think about, and whether what you are thinking about fits who you are and who you are becoming—or who you're being transformed by God to become. You have the ability, with God's help, to "[take] every thought captive to the obedience of Christ" (2 Corinthians 10:5b). As Ken Boa says, "Though we aren't responsible for every thought that enters our heads, we are responsible for what we do with them."[150]

Now that you know you're in control of what you think about, what are you going to do with this power?

Food for Thought

God himself is the primary source of all truth. The Scriptures often describe God's word as the best "food for thought." Peter said, "like newborn babies, long for the pure milk of the word, so that by it you may grow" (1 Peter 2:2). But we're not to stay on a milk-only diet. Paul chastises the Corinthian church for not being ready to receive the solid food of deeper teachings (1 Corinthians 3:2). Jesus himself said that doing God's will—communicated through his word—was like food for him (John 4:34).

These dietary metaphors reinforce the truth of Deuteronomy 6:6-9, that we need to consume God's truth with the frequency of daily meals. And, we need to expect his truth to cause us to grow in our thinking. We start out with spiritual baby food, but we must quickly move to chewier, more nutritious and diverse cuisine if we're going to grow (Hebrews 5:12). We study and learn and memorize and meditate on the Scriptures so we can comprehend increasingly complex and challenging truths.

The God who made the universe has more to teach us than we can imagine. Our increasingly powerful telescopes and microscopes are always discovering that God's creation is both bigger and smaller than anyone thought before. Why would we expect that learning the teachings of God would be easy, like being in a kindergarten class? Or that a few minutes spent in the Word once a week would be enough to help us think like the God who packed so much data into DNA that a single cell could become a firefly, a fish, or a farmer? As Finney famously said,

> "My brother, sister, friend—read, study, think, and read again. You were made to think. It will do you good to think; to develop your powers by study. God designed that religion should require thought, intense thought, and should thoroughly develop our powers of thought. The Bible itself is written in a style so condensed as to require much intense study. I do not pretend to so explain theology as to dispense with the labor of thinking. I have no ability and no wish to do so."[151]

What can you do to feed your mind with more of God's word each day?

Gift of Reading

If we could remember the sacrifices made over the centuries to make it possible for us to read the Scriptures ourselves, we would not take it for granted. Leaders like Wycliffe and Luther and the founders of Harvard College would be turning in their graves if they saw today's devaluing of literacy. Oppressors often keep education away from those they seek to enslave, which is why women and slaves in many cultures were (and are) prevented from learning to read. Today, many people's minds are locked from the inside, rusted shut by the lack of time spent reading.

But not us. We are going to use the gift of reading to set time aside each day to read the Bible. I find it's best to do this first thing each day. There are many plans available for reading the Scriptures at whatever pace you are comfortable. If you're new to the Bible, you might start with the New Testament so you can focus on what is most relevant to you today, then go back into the Old Testament with the context of Christ in view.

While reading plans help keep you moving forward, they can also hold you back from really understanding what you're reading. If you're too worried about getting through three or four chapters a day, then you can easily miss a profound thought. Sometimes a single verse can be enough to process for a day if you're really digging into it. Don't rush yourself if you don't understand something. If you're reading every day, it's not a failure to not complete your plan in a year. Just read the Bible every day.

One of the many gems of wisdom I received from my mentor, Dr. Timothy Barnett, was that with a Bible and an exhaustive concordance, I could be a Bible scholar. A concordance lists every word in the Bible in alphabetical order, along with every verse where each word appears. If you want to know where "love" appears in the Bible, look it up in the concordance and you'll see every love-filled verse. Most exhaustive concordances also include links to the original Hebrew or

Greek, providing a window into a richness of meaning that isn't captured in English, along with enlightening those who study them to the challenges involved in translating ancient sacred texts.

Speaking of translations, it's important to choose a version of the Bible that is as faithful to the original as possible. While the original words are certainly "God-breathed" (2 Timothy 3:16 NIV), translations are often biased to certain doctrinal perspectives, so it's helpful to understand where the translators are coming from. As English readers, we are blessed with dozens of translations. Because I'm a word nerd, I prefer word-for-word translations like NASB or ESV, but other phrase-by-phrase or even paraphrase versions can be more readable. As long as you're OK with the translator's doctrinal commitments, you'll do well with almost any of the leading versions. Ultimately, the best Bible version is the one you will *actually* read.

If you're willing to invest more time in focused study, the inductive method taught by Kay Arthur's Precept Ministries is outstanding.[152] Rather than telling you what someone thinks the Bible teaches, inductive study leads you in a process of letting the Bible speak for itself. You immerse yourself in the text, highlighting and cross-referencing and looking up words in dictionaries and concordances to get a full understanding. Inductive study takes time, but it is richly worthwhile.

If you're going to turn the tables on the influence of cultural messages in your life, you're going to have to read the Scriptures and focus on them with the frequency of Deuteronomy 6:6-9. Your focused diligence will be *so* worth it. You'll be certain to experience God's positive transformation because he promises:

> But from there you will seek the Lord your God, and you will find Him if you search for Him with your heart and all your soul (DEUTERONOMY 4:29).

Memorizing

One of the most effective ways to be transformed by the Scriptures is to commit them to memory. I've had more "ah-ha" moments while memorizing the Bible than I have through studying it in any other way. Insights I never noticed and details I didn't see as important have become vital to me as I've embedded the Bible into my mind.

Holding the Scriptures in your memory is like the best savings account ever. By depositing more of the Bible into your memory "account," you can make withdrawals when you need them. Answers to all of life's problems, wisdom for every decision, inspiration for every discouragement, and truth against every lie of the evil one is found in the Scriptures. If your memory account is filled with answers, wisdom, inspiration, and truth, you'll be ready to face whatever comes, and empowered to move forward into all God has for you.

Are you afraid? "For God hath not given us a spirit of fear, but of power, and of love, and of a sound mind" (2 Timothy 1:7 KJV). Lonely? "I will never desert you, nor will I ever forsake you" (Hebrews 13:5). Worried? "Be anxious for nothing, but in everything by prayer and supplication with thanksgiving let your requests be made known to God. And the peace of God, which surpasses all comprehension, will guard your hearts and your minds in Christ Jesus" (Philippians 4:6-7). Struggling with temptation? "He has granted to us His precious and magnificent promises, so that by them you may become partakers of the divine nature, having escaped the corruption that is in the world by lust" (2 Peter 1:4).

Like having an emergency fund when bad things happen, a mind full of the Scripture is a resource that pays the highest dividends. But people push back against this idea with excuses such as, "I don't have a good memory," or I'm not good at memorizing," or "I don't have time to memorize." As the French say, *au contraire, mon ami.*

If you believe you can't memorize the Bible for any reason, may I encourage you to renew your mind. What you say about yourself, even when untrue, can become true *if you live as though it were true.* If you tell yourself the lie that you don't have a good memory or that you don't have time, then you'll make decisions based on those lies and they will end up being true. Be *very* careful about anything you say about yourself.

Why do I say this? Because here's what I know: unless you have some bona-fide illness, you have a great memory. You remember all kinds of things that are important to you. You remember music, movie lines, and many events of the past. Sure, you might be so busy you don't know where your keys are half the time, but that's actually not because of a bad memory; it's probably because you're distracted, and you haven't formed the habit of putting your keys in the same place every day.

I've memorized several chapters of the Bible in addition to many verses. And I'm very busy with the many responsibilities I have from all the hats I wear. But because I've found the Scriptures so transformational, I've made memorization a priority in my life. That's how I know you can too.

If you don't think you can memorize or that you don't have time, let me tell you the story of Andrea. Her dad, Pastor Luke Veldt, led his church through a two-year journey of memorizing the longest chapter in the Bible, Psalm 119. They memorized all 176 verses, eight verses a month for 22 months. At the time, Andrea was 10 years old. And she has Down syndrome. As you can understand, Pastor Luke didn't expect his daughter to keep up with the rest of the church, but he wanted her to participate anyway.

But guess what? Andrea memorized Psalm 119. *All of it.* With random access to the verses. Like you could ask her, "What does verse 35 say," and she'd say, "Make me walk in the path of Your commands, for I delight in it."

Pastor Luke says this of his sweet daughter, "Andrea is pretty good at memorizing, but she does not have an extraordinary aptitude for it. She's not a genius or an autistic savant or something. She's just worked very hard at this, and had fun with it, too."[153]

So how did Andrea memorize all 176 verses of Psalm 119, with nearly 2,400 often repetitive words, complexities, depth of wisdom, and richness? Even with her extra challenges?

In a word, *intentionality.*

The Veldts practiced Deuteronomy 6 like I've never seen. They invented games. They wrote songs. They offered regular rewards and prizes for milestones. They talked about Psalm 119 when walking to school and when sitting at home. They wrote verses on whiteboards in their home, gradually erasing words. They made it fun, and worked very hard. As a result, they have filled their memory accounts with an investment of some of the most powerful words of love for God and his Word.

The Veldt's posted a video of Andrea playing one of the games on their website at http://memorizepsalm119.com/andrea/. I get choked up every time I see her do it.

Some of the most powerful parts of Psalm 119 are the repetitive declarations that start with "I." These are intended to renew the mind of the memorizer. "I shall not forget Your word." "I shall delight in your statues." "I will walk at liberty, for I seek your precepts." "I shall delight in your commandments, which I love." "Oh how I love Your law! It is my meditation all the day." The impact of memorizing these, of saying these things about yourself with a surrendered and open heart toward God, is that they end up becoming true. You become transformed by renewing your mind.

You *can* memorize the Scriptures. You'll need intentionality, a process, and you'll need to make it a priority. But memorization will change your thinking like nothing else. Combined with the power of the Holy Spirit, your renewed mind will start to think God's thoughts like never before, and your life will take a turn in a wonderful new direction.

Battle for Your Mind

Do you remember in chapter 3, how we learned that arch-propagandist Edward Bernays said that society needs to be "regimented" by shaping public opinion through an "invisible government?" He knew what we often forget: that the battle for our lives is waged on the field of our minds. The enemy of our souls—the father of lies—knows that if he lies to us long enough, we will live our lives based on those lies. That's why it's so important to renew our minds with God's truth.

Martial artists know that if they're going to be ready for battle, they have to practice. They repeatedly practice their blocks, kicks, and punches, in sophisticated combinations called *katas* or forms. When performing a *kata*, the student imagines various attackers and responds in an almost choreographed dance. This is why individuals who have earned a black belt can appear to move faster than people who haven't: they've anticipated responses to nearly every attack and their bodies just immediately move to defend themselves and immobilize their attackers.

There is an even more threatening battle for our minds, and it's fought every day as we're constantly pummeled with attacks that challenge reality itself. We can end up believing that up is down if we fill our minds with the constant stream of messaging and entertainment that comes across our screens. But those who are willing to do the hard work of studying and immersing themselves in God's Word can achieve a black-belt level of competency with God's truth. We can have our "powers of discernment trained by constant practice to distinguish good from evil" (Hebrews 5:14b ESV).

God has designed us to learn his ways through focused effort. We must seek him with all our heart (Jeremiah 29:13). And when we do, we *will* find him.

With yielded hearts, being changed by ongoing repentance, and becoming transformed by renewing our minds, we are ready to form new habits to replace those that may have been holding us back. By forming positive habits, our lives will take on a strength of purpose and character that will enable us to flourish in a world of harmful habit-forming screens. The next chapter will help us intentionally develop those positive habits.

CHAPTER 10

[UN]DISCIPLINED

PRACTICE #4: REPLACE HARMFUL HABITS WITH HELPFUL ONES

Are Habits Destiny?

> But solid food is for the mature, for those who have their powers of discernment trained by constant practice to distinguish good from evil. Hebrews 5:14 (ESV)

> "It was the sixteenth-century scholar Erasmus who said, 'A nail is driven out by another nail; habit is overcome by habit.'" —ZIG ZIGLAR[154]

If your brain was a city, what would be the most valuable neighborhood? Where would developers pay top dollar to build gated communities lined with million-dollar homes? Would it be your central nervous system? Your fight or flight instinct? Your higher reasoning? Maybe your long-term memory?

Nope. None of the above. The part of your brain that powerful companies and spiritual forces invest in more than any other is the *habit-forming system*. Those investors know the power of habits, and are willing to pay almost any price to develop yours.

Habits are powerful because they are automatic, almost unconscious behaviors. We don't have to think about our habitual actions—we just act. Sometimes we notice that we're acting out of habit, but most of the time we are oblivious to those actions.

But there was a time when every one of your habits was not automatic at all. How you eat, get dressed, brush your teeth, walk, drive, speak, or write was something you learned to do, often with difficulty. Every parent or babysitter who has taught a child to feed themselves or tie their own shoes knows how hard it is to learn some of the very basic things we do instinctually today.

And that's great news! If your habits are taking you off track, even if those habits are implanted by intentionally habit-forming screen content, those habits can be changed. They may have a powerful grip on you today, but their grip can be loosened, and eventually you can let go of them altogether. It won't be easy, but you can, and must, change some of your habits in order to find the free and purposeful life you've been made to live.

Matthew Kelly says that habits are so powerful they offer an almost prophetic view into what your life will be like in the future.

> Thoughts create actions. Actions create habits. Habits create character. And your character is your destiny—in the workplace and in relationships. In every sphere of life, your character provides significant insight into your future. [. . .] Habits are the building blocks of character. What are the things you do every day, every week, or every month? **If you can tell me what your habits are, I can tell you what your future looks like.**[155]

Anytime someone claims to be able to tell the future, I'm skeptical. But Kelly's claim to predict your future by considering your habits isn't like reading a horoscope. It's more like reading a map. If you get on a road and keep going the same way, the map will predict your destination.

Blaise Pascal said, "The strength of a man's virtue should not be measured by his special exertions, but by his habitual acts."[156] What we do every day matters much more than what we rarely do. If we want a life filled with what God calls good, wise, and virtuous, we must focus on our habits, and change those that are pulling us off track.

Author and teacher Preston Sprinkle nailed it in a podcast entitled, "Can you be porn free with an iPhone?" He said, "Building up patterns and rhythms and habits of discipline and desires for holiness is the only way to live towards righteousness in a sin-saturated world."[157]

Are your habits taking you where you really want to go? Are they reinforcing the biblical practices you've already learned, encouraging daily surrender, freedom, and the continual renewing of your mind? If not, this is a great time to replace those habits with new habits that reinforce your intentional life.

Habit Forming

Neuroscientists are discovering a lot more about the way our brains create and process habits. They have found that our brains use a lot of energy when we're doing something new or challenging, but habits don't require much brainpower. We know this already. All of us feel physically tired after working on mentally difficult problems, but chores like folding clothes or cleaning dishes can tend to relax our minds.

Charles Duhigg wrote a hugely popular book on this subject called *The Power of Habit*. He shares detailed research about how habits are formed and how they can be changed. Duhigg's three-step *habit loop* is a simpler version of the four-step process we saw in Nir Eyal's *Hooked* in chapter 2. Duhigg boils habit forming down to: a *cue*, a *routine*, and a *reward*. He explains:

> First, there is a cue, a trigger that tells your brain to go into automatic mode and which habit to use. Then there is the routine, which can be physical or mental or emotional. Finally, there is a reward, which helps your brain figure out if this particular loop is worth remembering for the future.[158]

Duhigg says the cue and reward end up becoming intertwined over time, creating a craving or anticipation. The power driving the habit is the craving that immediately follows the cue. The problem is that our habit-forming cue-crave system doesn't care whether what we end up doing habitually is valuable or worthwhile. It's all about how good the reward feels—the better it feels, the stronger the habit. The industries and forces behind our screen content know this, and use habit cycles masterfully to manipulate our desires.

So if our boredom cue fires, our routine is to pick up our phone, because the apps have so effectively manipulated our reward system that we can't be bored—we *crave* the distraction. If our loneliness cue fires, we might find a quick fix with pornography. The brain thinks, "loneliness solved, do that again." And the spiritual forces that use our habit cycles against us mock us as we fall for trap after trap.

Habits formed by screens are more dangerous because of the tight, fast, and coordinated feedback loops involved in the reward system. Where the cue-routine-reward cycle for something like food can span minutes or even hours, the same cycle is measured in milliseconds when driven by a screen.

Bestselling author and speaker Stephen Mansfield shared a helpful metaphor about how habits are formed in a podcast entitled "Habits and the Brain."[159] Picture a pristine field of tall, golden wheat, blowing gently in the wind, ready for harvest. Imagine walking through that wheat field along a meandering path from one side to the other. If you returned to your starting point the next day, you might have a hard time seeing the path you originally walked through the field. But if you were to walk the same way again, the next day the trail would be a little clearer. Take the same path every day for a month, and the field would have an obvious trail of packed dirt.

Our brains record habits in a similar way. Over time and with repetition, the cue-routine-reward cycle creates entrenched patterns in the brain. Once cued, we barely have to think about the routine be-cause the data has been stored deep within the habit-forming system.

The "Way" of Habits in the Bible

The Bible calls us to fill our lives with good habits. The plea to walk in good habits is often made with the word "way," like the habitual path through our wheat field above. Proverbs 16:7 says, "When a man's **ways** are pleasing to the LORD, He makes even his enemies to be at peace with him." Jeremiah exhorts people to "[t]urn now everyone from his evil **way** and from the evil of your deeds" (Jeremiah 25:5). In that last verse, the International Standard Version translates "way"— the Hebrew word *deh-rek*[160]—as "habits."

God cries out to the habitually idol-worshiping Israelites with an offer of a different "way":

> Thus says the Lord,
> "Stand by the ways
> and see
> and ask
> for the ancient paths,
> Where *the good way is*,
> and walk in it;
> And you will find rest for your souls"
> (JEREMIAH 6:16, emphasis added).

The Lord calls us to "stand by the **ways** [plural of *deh-rek*] and see and ask." We are to look from a distance at possible ways to habitually fill our lives, and ask for wisdom. It's like a world of habits lays in front us, each with consequences. God doesn't want us to just jump in and try out each *way*, because he knows some habits leave scars. While we may break free, we are never the same as if we had never tried them. God can certainly redeem anything, but total healing for the damage inflicted by some habits will have to wait until Heaven. That's why God wants us to *see* and *ask* first.

Notice we are to "ask for the ancient paths, where the good way is," and if we do that, we "will find rest for our souls." That *rest* is what Jesus promises in Matthew 11:29 when he invites us to "take My yoke upon you and learn from Me, for I am gentle and humble in heart, and YOU WILL FIND REST FOR YOUR SOULS." The NASB capitalizes those last seven words to show that Jesus is quoting Jeremiah 6:16. This soul-rest offered by God through Christ is in opposition to the angsty, striving, fear-filled paths taken by those who follow the way of destructive habits.

In Christ, the good *way* is the path of constant, moment-by-moment, surrendered obedience to him as Lord. Jesus said, "I am the way, and the truth, and the life; no one comes to the Father but through

Me" (John 14:6). We often hear about Jesus as the *way* to God in the context of eternal salvation, which is true. But I think Jesus intends a deeper meaning. His *way* is to become the habitual focus of our lives. In fact, the original believers weren't even called "Christians," but were known as followers of "the Way" (Acts 9:2).

So the New testament calls us to a *way*, even *The Way*. But how do we find the *way* of good habits?

After scolding his readers because of their immaturity, the author of Hebrews says: "But solid food is for the mature, for those who have their powers of discernment trained by constant practice to distinguish good from evil" (Hebrews 5:14 ESV). Constant practice. The Greek word is *hexis*,[161] which is literally Greek for "habit." Those who develop good habits "have their senses trained," where "trained" is *gegymnasmena*,[162] which is where we get "gym" or "gymnasium."

Can you see it? Good habits come from the kind of intensity, focus, and discipline we see in a professional athlete. Or the skilled musician who practices over and over for years until she can play beautifully without hardly thinking about it. Or the black belt who has so mastered his martial art he doesn't even have to think about what he'll do if someone tries to punch him. Good habits are built up over time as we *repeatedly practice them.*

Because what we do over and over matters. It shapes who we are and who we become—the *way* we go. You can see why parents are commanded to "train up a child in the **way** he should go" (Proverbs 22:6). We are to lead our kids into practices that will take them— habitually—in God's good way. We are also to keep our children—and ourselves—from practicing things that take us off track.

Going a Different Way

All of us have habits that, like a well-worn pathway off a cliff, aren't taking us where we really want to go. But we've practiced many of those habits for years, so the trail is beaten down, even if it's in the wrong direction. It's just so easy to keep doing those old habits. But they can be overcome if we will not only stop going down the old ways, but also intentionally replace those old habits with new, good habits.

Stopping a bad habit without replacing it with a good one is like clearing a field without planting new seeds—it will quickly fill with weeds. But when we replace our bad habits with good ones, the cleared field will produce the crop we're hoping for. Author, teacher, and ministry leader Ken Boa says it this way:

> Maybe you've noticed that habits shape a person. They come to define someone's character and overall disposition. When we develop habits of godliness, they shape our attitude and our approach toward the world. The habits of our sinful nature get replaced by habits in keeping with our new, redeemed nature—giving us a whole new disposition.[163]

Charles Duhigg agrees that bad habits must be replaced, and says people must follow a "golden rule" of habit change to be successful. His golden rule lines up with his three-step habit loop. He says,

> To change a habit, you must keep the old cue, and deliver the old reward, but insert a new routine. That's the [golden] rule: If you use the same cue, and provide the same reward, you can shift the routine and change the habit. Almost any behavior can be transformed if the cue and reward stay the same.[164]

For example, if an alcoholic is cued to drink by stress or worry, and the routine of drinking rewards him with relief, then, Duhigg says, Alcoholics Anonymous follows his golden rule. Among other things, AA replaces the routine of drinking with a routine of frequent meetings and one-on-one mentoring. So the cue of stress or worry is rewarded with relief, but that relief comes through a different habitual routine.

This is a helpful way to think about replacing habits, but it has drawbacks too. Duhigg's claim is that you can't actually eliminate a bad habit, because the cues and rewards are always there. And for relatively broad cues like "worry" or "boredom" or "stress," and a reward of "relief," that may be partially true. There are always problems that can serve as cues to entice us into craving some kind of relief.

However, many habits have harmful cues and even more harmful rewards. All three parts of Duhigg's habit loop need to be replaced for those habits, and I believe they can be.

For example, someone might be a compulsive TV watcher because they don't want to deal with the dysfunctional family relationships they have at home. So the cue in that case would be difficult relationships. The reward is avoidance. All three parts of that habit cycle are harmful, and need to be replaced. Likewise, a person might be cued by Instagram to be jealous of a friend's vacations or possessions, so they spend money they don't have for the reward of keeping up with them. The jealousy, overspending, and comparison all need to be replaced.

As you evaluate your bad habits, it's very important to get very honest about what is cueing or triggering them. Why are you *really* always on your phone? Are you avoiding something? Hiding from some pain? Driven by jealousy? Fear of missing out (FOMO)? Or just procrastinating? If you will pray, "search me, O God, and know my heart," and seek the wisdom of trusted advisors, then God will help you find the deeper reasons for your habits so you can overcome them.

If your habits are triggered by deep wounds, you may need professional counseling to really get to the bottom of your struggle. Some people just can't learn why they have self-destructive habits without help, and that's totally okay. If that's you, a counselor can help you dig in and find out what's really going on. I've been blessed with very helpful Christian counselors who have helped me look honestly into my past hurts and find true healing. Their insight, and the life change that can come with it, is completely worth their cost and time.

The Essential Power of God

Since Scripture calls us to a life filled with habits that lead us in God's *way*, it's no surprise that the key to success is the One who is calling us, God himself. We must trust God to be the power that fills every part of our lives, especially as it involves supplying the power to replace bad habits with good ones.

One of the most powerful habit replacing verses is 2 Peter 1:3-4, which says,

> His divine power has granted to us everything pertaining
> to life and godliness, through the true knowledge of Him
> who called us by His own glory and excellence. For by
> these He has granted to us His precious and magnificent
> promises, so that by them you may become partakers of
> the divine nature, having escaped the corruption that is
> in the world by lust.

This is a great passage to memorize. It has been critical mind-renewing fuel from God to help me overcome many bad habits. Did you see the power of this truth? God has already given us all we need for life and godliness, even habitual godliness. He has given us *everything* we need to be like him! That is a promise to receive, trust, and accept.

The way we receive God's divine power is by constantly abiding in Christ (John 15:1-5). We are given the Holy Spirit to lead us into all truth (John 16:13). As we renew our minds with these truths and apply them to any habit we need to overcome, we will find the power of God helping us to do things we could never do on our own.

The reason I'm sharing Christ-centered biblical practices instead of more secular solutions (that might have a broader market reach) is because this is *my* story. The only reason I've been able to break free from sins and addictions and bad habits is because God has done a great work in and through me, helping and teaching and empowering me to overcome. Millions of other believers share similar stories. I encourage you to continue to trust the One who is "the *way,* the truth, and the life." Walking in his *way,* not flawlessly, but habitually, is the path to the freedom and purpose God wants for all of us.

Directions to New Ways

There are so many different habits that detailing examples to consider could fill a whole book. However, since space is limited, I'll share a few of my most helpful ideas here. We will, of course, focus on our habits with screens, but these principles apply to other habits as well. I encourage you to think about your screen and non-screen habits as you read the following ideas.

Win the Morning

Who sets the agenda for your day? The first words of the morning win. That's why morning news shows are ready first thing to get you worked up about whatever is most profitable for the media corporations. And it's why smartphone apps are set up with notifications and carefully designed rewards to trigger habit-forming loops in the brain. All of these things are intentionally designed to capture your morning.

Your morning habits are a critical part of what will determine the quality of your relationship with God and others during the course of the day. If you let the culture set your agenda through screens, then you will become just as angry and worried and self-focused and distracted as everyone else. But if you start with a morning habit of prayer, Bible study, exercise, and planning, your life will be filled with much more peace, productivity, and joy.

When I got my first smartphone, I found myself drawn to check email first thing every morning. It became a bad habit, crowding out my thoughts about anything important. So, in alignment with Deuteronomy 6:6-9, I decided to let God set the agenda for my morning with a very intentional quiet-time process that has become a habit over many years now. My morning routine has grown over the years, one small change at a time.

As you consider building new habits into your life, don't feel like you have to adopt everything all at once. Change one habit at a time. Let each new change become almost automatic before you add the next. Over time, you'll look back and be grateful for the positive changes you see and especially for the positive results.

If your work requires deep thought, like strategic planning, writing, or composing, you would do well to go further and adopt a practice of "monk mode morning." Cal Newport, author of *Deep Work*, describes this idea on his outstanding blog. "The execution of the monk mode morning is straightforward. Between when you wake up and noon: no meetings, no calls, no text, no email, no Slack, no Internet. You simply work deeply on something (or some things) that matter."[165]

I like the clarity and simplicity of the concept, and encourage you to add it as a habitual routine, even if only once or twice a week. Even if you don't go all-in on "monk mode," you can intentionally choose to disconnect from everything that's potentially distracting while you're focusing on whatever is important at the moment, for whatever period you decide.

Pre-made Decisions

One of the best parts of my morning routine are the pre-made decisions that form the habits of my daily practice. Pre-made decisions are the most powerful, because you make them at a time when you're at your best, and when you're focused on your highest priorities and values.

I decided not to check any online input before breakfast, which comes after my quiet time and exercise. I just don't do that. As a result I don't have to ask myself every morning whether or not I should check my email or social media from bed. That decision is made.

At first, when checking my email from bed was one of my habits, I had to make other changes to replace it. I had to move my phone off my nightstand so I couldn't reach it when my "gotta check it" cue fired. Today, it's not a temptation because my morning routine is so engrained. If you want to follow the same practice, you might need to keep your phone out of your room altogether. Also, be sure to shut down all notifications overnight, and disable most notifications the rest of the day. These decisions will close the door on content-delivery engineers who want to distract you during the day, and will keep you more focused on what really matters.

What decisions do you need to make to lead you to become the best version of yourself—one who is surrendered to God and following his ways? Decide to make those decisions in advance, so that when circumstances arise, you don't have to wonder or agonize about what you're going to do. You won't be as tempted to cross certain lines, because you've already decided.

Micro-Habits

Many of our habits are tiny feedback loops of a few seconds or less. Waiting for five seconds leads our minds to wonder what's happening online. Seeing the TV when we walk in the house cues us to turn it on. Our response to each of these cues is habitual, so we'll have to replace these habits if we want to overcome them.

One part of replacing a habit, especially when you're just getting started, is to make going through the routine of the habit more difficult. If you're working and you're tempted to check Twitter whenever you have five seconds to wait on something, then you need to make it harder to get on Twitter. Delete the app from your phone, or sign out from your computer so you will have to sign in to check it. If seeing a TV makes you want to turn it on, then you might need to move the TV somewhere else, put it in a cabinet, or take the bold step to get rid of it altogether. If online temptations keep snagging you, then you might need to install some accountability software like Covenant Eyes to help you break the habitual pull.

One vital replacement for bad micro-habits in my life has been a combination of gratitude—praise—and Scripture memory. When I'm tempted, I now habitually say something like this in my head, "Lord, thank you that you have set me free from this, and have given me everything I need for life and godliness" (2 Peter 1:3). It's amazing how quickly thanking God for the truth of his power and grace in my life switches my thinking. When I'm bored, I am developing habits of practicing the presence of God like we talked about in chapter 7. A quick prayer, recognizing God's presence and love and inviting him to direct my thinking is a much better use of five seconds than the distraction of the next text, tweet or email.

Virtuous Habits

In their excellent book *A Practical Guide To Culture*, John Stonestreet and Brett Kunkle talk about the need to develop habits of virtue. We hear so much about the opposite—habits of vice—that even the idea of virtuous habits is surprising. But they can be developed.

For example, what do you do when you see a dirty job that needs to be done? Is your first habitual thought, "someone (else) should do something about that?" What if, instead, you were the first one to habitually take out the trash? Or to pick up that litter from the road? Or to wipe off that counter? While you certainly don't want to spend your whole life cleaning up after other people who should be helping too, if you develop a positive habit to act instead of complain, you'll bless those around you and be happier yourself.

How do you react when you hear something offensive? What if someone insults you—on purpose? Or if they cut you off in traffic? Your responses to these triggers are habits too. If you're cued by being mistreated, first remember what Jesus said, "bless those who curse you, pray for those who mistreat you" (Luke 6:28). A hard command, right? But a command nonetheless. A virtuous habit can be formed by first preparing for it. When you're likely to be in a situation where you might be offended, decide how you'll bless the offender in advance. The reward you'll receive for your genuinely positive response will be much better than if you escalate offenses with more offenses.

Win the Night

Good habits around your nighttime routine are critical for arriving at each new day in your best state of mind. If you're regularly in the habit of watching TV until you fall asleep, you're likely not getting enough rest—which, as we saw in chapter 1, is the Netflix CEO's stated goal. Plus, you're leaving yourself open to manipulation by intentionally desire-shaping messages at the very time you're most vulnerable.

I encourage you to make a habit to set a time—at least an hour before you plan to go to sleep—to shut down entertainment-focused screens. Even better, limit entertainment screen time to once or twice a week. I've found it helpful if I don't check email or social media for 30-60 minutes before I plan to go to sleep. In doing so, I've created an intentional online-input blackout from well before sleep until after breakfast. Instead, I focus on family time or reading positive, typically Christian or wisdom-focused reading—good food for nighttime thought.

When our kids lived at home, even into high school, we had a nighttime ritual of reading an inspiring book and praying together. Those nights of traveling to Narnia, reliving the stories of brave foreign missionaries, or hearing from the *Book of Virtues* were some of our favorite times. No devices. No distractions. Just Dad or Mom reading, often followed by great questions and discussions. Even now, as empty nesters, my wife and I read a book together several nights a week. It's a happy habit we look forward to, and one that keeps us unplugged, free, and ready to be our best in the morning.

Putting Moses To Work For You

As we saw in chapter 9, Deuteronomy 6 commands us to talk about God's ways every morning, every night, at meals, while driving, and to keep them always visible. Instead of letting our screens fill those times for us, it's time to build habits that take us to the good place our Maker intends.

While you work to replace old habits with new ones, remember that each habit you want to change has an almost magnetic pull. Replacing habits is less like flipping a switch and more like turning an ocean liner. That's why we must bring all of God's power and all of our disciplined intentionality to the challenge. As Dave Ramsey often reminds us in this old quote, "Work like it all depends on you, and pray like it all depends on God." We need both: God, and everything we can give.

The intentional life is, by definition, a self-disciplined life. Even if you consider yourself more of a free spirit, you will only be truly free if you can overcome any habits that are keeping you from experiencing the freedom you long for. Thankfully, self-control is one of the fruit of the Spirit of Galatians 5. The power of God will help us grow into the life of discipline God uses to set us free.

Keeping a daily journal is one way to help reinforce your self-discipline as you embark on your habit-changing journey. List those habits God shows you to replace, and think about what good habits should replace them. Then, one by one, focus on replacing a particular negative habit with a positive replacement until it becomes automatic. Keep track of your journey, so that in the months and years to come, you can look back on your progress. You'll be encouraged by all God does in your life, and see the fruit of following in his good *way*.

To keep you focused, remember Matthew Kelly's insightful quote: "If you can tell me what your habits are, I can tell you what your future looks like."[166] We all hope for an awesome future. We want to become all God made us to be, unhindered by anything that would hold us back.

After beginning a path to upgrade your habits, you're ready to learn biblical practice number five—the pursuit of your personal calling. God wants us to become free from every entanglement so we can join him on his mission to bless the world with his message of freedom in Christ. Each one of us has a unique part to play in God's mission, especially prepared by God (Ephesians 2:10). By pursuing your God-given calling, your life will be filled with new joy and excitement as you watch God work through you to impact others.

CHAPTER 11

[UN]MOTIVATED

PRACTICE #5: USE YOUR FREEDOM TO PURSUE YOUR CALLING

You Have a God-Given Purpose

> For we are His workmanship, created in Christ Jesus for good works, which God prepared beforehand so that we would walk in them (EPHESIANS 2:10).

> "To live out my calling, I must first believe that God has a calling and purpose for my life, and that I need to actively engage in finding and developing that calling."
> —TODD WILSON[167]

Who am I? Why am I here? Is there a purpose to this life? These are questions we all ask at some point in our lives, often more than once. At those big life-defining milestones like graduating, getting married, having kids, then seeing those kids graduate and get married (quicker than you may imagine), we think about whether our life has a purpose, and if we're on track. Certainly, not everyone shares the same milestones, but we all share the hope to live a life that makes a difference.

But in a world often filled with despair, hopelessness, and soul-crushing trials, purpose can be lost. Many people find themselves wandering aimlessly through life because they don't see any possible way to make a difference in such a messed-up world. For others, the struggle to put food on the table and a roof over their head makes the idea of a meaningful life feel extravagant.

Screen-saturation fuels a purpose-draining sense of hopelessness. Constant noise keeps us from even thinking about impacting the world. The best some people do in the face of a world filled with unrest, divisiveness, poverty, war, corruption, crime, and darkness is to complain on social media, "Someone should do something about this!"

Technology also fights against real-world purpose when it becomes a virtual purpose substitute. Social media and video games can feed our longing for purpose by making us *feel* like we're accomplishing something meaningful—by design. For some of the more addicted gamers, every fight against an electronic foe satiates their inborn hunger to make a difference, leaving them unequipped and unmotivated to battle real-world enemies and rescue truly hurting people.

Even inspiring stories risk demotivating our search for purpose— if we consume too many of them—whether through books, television, or movies. We are rightly thrilled when Luke Skywalker rescues his father, or when Frodo says, "it's done." And as we saw in chapter 6, stories like these help us see what's possible and expand our vision, igniting our motivation. But like any good thing, too much of any one thing becomes harmful. If we only consume these stories and never live out the greater story of the life we've been given, we're missing the point.

Given that the quest for purpose is common to every person, and there are many forces allied against us finding and living out our purpose, we can draw two conclusions. First, the desire for purpose is God-given. Our Creator made us not just for survival, but for true significance. And second, there is a real spiritual battle working to keep us from discovering and fulfilling our purpose. The principalities and powers we explored in chapter 4 are bent on *stealing, killing,* and *destroying* us, especially our motivation to make a lasting difference in the lives of others.

If you ever question whether your life has a purpose beyond the next paycheck or crisis, renew your mind with the truth of Scripture.

After Paul tells us in Ephesians 2:8 that we have been saved by grace through faith, he goes on to tell us what we have been saved to *do:*

> For we are **His workmanship**, created in Christ Jesus **for good works**, which God prepared beforehand so that we would walk in them (EPHESIANS 2:10, emphasis mine).

The word "workmanship" is the Greek word *poiéma*, which is the root of the English word "poem." God exercised more care, imagination, and creativity when he made us *in his image* than Shakespeare poured into his poetic sonnets. And we are masterfully created by God in Christ to accomplish good things in the world. God *prepared* our good purpose *beforehand*. That's why we all seek purpose—it's built in by our Designer.

But what are the specific *good works* God intends for you to do? We will seek this answer soon.

First, consider: God has gone to a lot of trouble to set you free. He sent Jesus to rescue you, so that by your surrender to him you may break free from everything that would lead you off track. He gave you the Scriptures and his Spirit to teach you what needs to be removed from your life. His truth and goodness renew your mind, leading you to freedom—one new, good habit at a time. But to what end? Is it just for your benefit, so you'll have a happy life?

It's Not About You

That's right. We are called by God to walk in freedom so we can fulfill our God-given purpose. And our purpose is ultimately not to focus on ourselves at all.

Pastor Rick Warren begins chapter 1 of his mega-bestseller *The Purpose Driven Life* with these unforgettable words: "It's not about you."[168] That statement pulls the rug out from our natural inward focus. The quest to find our purpose isn't about navel-gazing self-fulfillment. It's found in focusing on the needs of others.

Our others-focused purpose is what pastor Andy Stanley calls "the catch." In an insightful podcast series, Stanley warns purpose seekers about the fine print at the bottom of the certificate of purpose we seek. It says, "purpose is about becoming a means to an end." If we are a *means to an end,* then we aren't the *end* ourselves. Just like everything in your home has a purpose—your toaster is for making toast, your towels are for drying things, and your pens are for writing—Stanley concludes, "the purpose of that item is *not* that item."[169]

We hear a lot these days about finding meaning. We're told how to find a meaningful job, a meaningful cause, or a meaningful community. And we saw in chapter 3 how Mark Zuckerberg is capitalizing on the idea of "meaning" by twisting it inward. But what is meaning, really? Meaning, as Stanley points out, is "about being a *means* to an end that's more or greater than yourself." He continues, "Meaning is like light to a bug. We are all attracted to it, but the closer we get, we realize what it's going to cost."[170] Finding true meaning means giving ourselves away for the benefit of other people.

Our quest for a meaningful purpose seems like a paradox. Purpose isn't about us, but on the other hand, it's the best way for us to live. *We are never happier than when we aren't focusing on ourselves.*

God always blesses us so we can be a blessing to others. Every hardship we overcome, by the grace of God, helps other people as we share what we've learned. And blessing others with what we've been given is a never-ending cycle, like "living waters" that never run dry (John 7:38). The more we share our lives through our God-given purpose, the more we feel fulfilled and encouraged, which fuels us up to bless even more people, over and over again.

Our others-focused purpose ends up being good for us—not because we seek our good, but because we seek the good of others. And there's another benefit of others-focused purpose: it motivates us to continue our biblical practices and avoid falling back into unintentional living. The former Israelite slaves found the same thing on their journey to the promised land.

But Purpose Helps You Anyway

During the Israelite's long journey to freedom, Moses was called by God to climb a mountain and receive the Ten Commandments. The former slaves were just supposed to wait for Moses to come back and share God's commands. But, as Professor Harold Hill says in *The Music Man*, "idle hands are the devil's playground."

Moses was gone a long time, and the people quickly grew tired of waiting around. So they started a popular Facebook group to share stories about what they thought had happened to Moses. Various conspiracy theories arose. One claimed an alien abduction, another said Moses snuck back to Egypt to run for Pharaoh. Facebook was as divisive in 2000 B.C. as it is today. But there was one thing they all agreed upon: waiting for Moses was b-o-r-i-n-g. So what did they do?

> Now when the people saw that Moses delayed to come down from the mountain, the people assembled about Aaron and said to him, "Come, make us a god who will go before us; as for this Moses, the man who brought us up from the land of Egypt, we do not know what has become of him" (EXODUS 32:1).

The people decided they needed something tangible to worship, so they talked Aaron into making a golden calf. Then they held an epic barbecue: as the Bible reports, "the people sat down to eat and to drink, and rose up to play" (Exodus 32:6).

Isn't that what we're tempted to do? Without a purpose, we naturally seek pleasure. We find shiny things to distract us, like the golden calf of old. Then we party around it. A lot. Our pleasure-seeking rituals often evolve into worship of the shiny thing, and become idolatry. And idolatry destroys us and everyone around us.

Seven chapters later, the people of the Exodus were completely different. God graciously renewed his covenant with the people, gave them his commands, and especially, gave very specific details about how they were to worship the one true God. He designed their new worship center, the tabernacle, with details down to the thread for the curtains and the number of hooks in the curtain rods. Every dimension, color, piece of furniture, and item of priestly clothing was carefully detailed in God's blueprint for the new center of worship.

And guess what? The people obeyed! The same wanderers who were partying with a golden calf before (well, minus those who were executed for their idolatry) now got on board with their new purpose. The Bible says,

> So the sons of Israel did all the work according to all that the LORD had commanded Moses. And Moses examined all the work and behold, they had done it; just as the LORD had commanded, this they had done. So Moses blessed them (EXODUS 39:42–43).

Quite a change from Moses's furious reaction when he came down the mountain and saw them worshiping the golden calf.

There are very few times in the Bible when we hear that the Israelites did everything they were supposed to do. Much of the time they were doing "what was right in [their] own eyes" (Judges 17:6). And mostly, what was right in their own eyes was to worship idols, which almost always involved food, drink, and other sensual pleasures. But their idolatry always ended very badly for them.

So what was the difference in Exodus 39? Why did these former slaves "do according to all that the LORD had commanded Moses?"

Could it be that they were motivated by their specific purpose— their unique mission from God? The establishment of their community, construction of their church, organization of their leadership, and scheduling of their daily, weekly, monthly, and yearly routines, all took a lot of time. And it was time spent doing the right things: what God wanted them to do.

By focusing on their God-given purpose, they were able to walk in the freedom God intended for them. God went to a whole lot of trouble to set them free from Egyptian slavery, and he wanted them to live in freedom. His purposes were designed to keep them on that path to freedom.

Do you see the parallels with our lives today? God has gone to a whole lot of trouble to set us free from everything that used to hold us back. He sent Jesus the Christ to live, die, and rise from the dead, then enthroned Christ at his right hand as King of kings. He has preserved the Scriptures by his Spirit over thousands of years so that "whosoever will" can learn, come, and surrender to the King.

The King then gives us all a purpose, a mission, an invitation to follow. We show our allegiance to the King by joining him in his mission. And as a helpful byproduct, we avoid the tempting idolatries that so often pull us away when we're not intentionally pursuing our purpose.

I've found this to be so true in my life. Among the things that keep me on track when I'm tempted is my sense of God's calling and purpose. I remember times when I've failed, gone off the rails, and regret the loss and waste of that time. I never want to experience that again. So I constantly keep my purpose in front of me. In fact, I think my sense of purpose is among the most powerful ways God keeps me following him as closely as I do. As I mentioned in chapter 8, I consider myself a "soldier in active service," so I can't get entangled in non-soldier behaviors if I'm going to "please the one who enlisted [me] as a soldier" (2 Timothy 2:4).

So, what is your God-given purpose? What is compelling enough to motivate you to live the rest of your life in joyful service to God and others? What calling will encourage you to habitually embrace positive and biblical practices in order to pursue it?

Discovering Your Purpose

Todd Wilson, CEO of Exponential and expert life-planning coach, wrote a *magnum opus* on discovering purpose. It's called *More: Find Your Personal Calling and Live Life to the Fullest Measure*. I'll share some highlights here to give you a glimpse of the path to discovering your purpose, and I encourage you to read Wilson's book to find depth and clarity around your calling.

You may have noticed how I've been using the terms *purpose* and *calling* interchangeably. I'm doing that on purpose (nice pun). Rick Warren linked the two words in a podcast interview with Wilson, saying, "A purpose-driven life and living your calling are identical."[171] The reason we're here—our God-given *purpose*—is what we are *called* by God to discover and pursue, for all of our lives.

As a former naval engineer, Wilson helps us answer our universal questions of purpose with a methodically organized process he calls the BE, DO, and GO framework. He says,

More provides a framework to tackle these questions head on. It starts with who we are, and that we are uniquely created with a unique identity and design. Who are we created to BE? This identity is one we actively discover and participate in activating. Our BE or identity overflows into and shapes our mission. What are we made to DO? Finally, our DO requires a context, or a position where it is lived out. Where are we to GO? [172]

Our identity (BE), or what Rick Warren calls our "shape," is critical in determining our calling. We all have natural God-given talents and are growing in skills enabled by our talents. God calls us to use what we've been given, not what we haven't been given. In the parable of the talents (Matthew 25:14-30), each person was only held responsible for what they did with the talents their master gave them, not what the others received. A violinist isn't called to be an excellent soccer player. In the movie *Chariots of Fire*, famed Olympic runner and missionary to China Eric Liddell says, "I believe God made me for a purpose, but he also made me fast. And when I run I feel His pleasure." You have built-in gifts that God wants you to offer to him as you seek your purpose, and when you do, you'll feel his pleasure too.

Our mission (DO) is what we are specifically called to do with the abilities we've been given. Like a bicycle, a pencil, or a guitar are useful for many purposes, we can apply our gifts and skills in many different ways. Someone gifted with an especially great voice might use it for radio, stage, music, teaching, preaching, leadership, or in many other ways only limited by imagination. A craftsman who knows how to build or repair homes might use his skill to help the poor, build churches, or design schools in developing countries. It's exciting to wonder how God might use our unique gifts in ways that surprise us. You'll see God's wisdom when you find yourself applying your gifts to *do* something you might never have planned.

Finally, God calls us to apply our gifts in certain ways at a particular time and place (GO). While we all may dream of deploying our purpose at some far-off and exotic locale, Wilson encourages us to start right where we are. There is nobody else who is made like you, who can do what you do, in the moment and location you are in right now. God may move you later, and we all need to be open to his leading. But the best place to start is here and now. As you apply your gifts toward doing specific things where you are, you'll become more effective and fruitful, and will see your impact grow.

Each part of Wilson's BE-DO-GO framework applies in two domains: our primary or general calling, and our secondary or unique calling.

All Christians share the primary calling, which is to "be disciples of Jesus who make disciples where we are."[173] We are to faithfully obey Jesus's great commission, to "go therefore and make disciples of all the nations" (Matthew 28:19). While that will look different in the life of a pastor than in the life of a pilot or pipe-fitter or programmer or physician or politician, we all share this common mission and are clearly called to participate in it. Each one of us is called to be discipled in the ways of Christ, and then to disciple others just like we've been discipled. This is our priority, and the calling we must seek to fulfill in our surrendered walk with God.

Our unique calling is what most of us think of when we ask, "Why am I here?" I've found the concept of our unique calling expressed by many authors as the convergence of two or three key ideas. Frederick Buechner said, "Purpose is the place where your deep gladness meets the world's needs."[174] Andy Stanley says that purpose is often found at the center of what breaks your heart, your gifts and skills, and the opportunities you're given. Wilson calls this our "sweet spot," which he says is "defined by the intersection of our unique identity, the good works [God] calls us to accomplish, and the place we are called to do it."[175]

Does the idea of living your life in your sweet spot excite you? Does the thought that you are uniquely made for a specific purpose in this time and place make you want to find it, and get started doing it? Of course, you may have to make changes over many years to set yourself up for maximum impact, all while being purposeful in your everyday life. I certainly had to make many critical decisions and changes. But the knowledge that God had something for me to do inspired me to overcome many obstacles, study intensely, adopt these practices, and pursue my calling with all my heart.

Purposeful Motives

Sometimes when we think of discovering our calling, we imagine something popular and prominent, like a marquee sign with our name in lights. And dreams of fame aren't necessarily bad, but they don't often form the most important part of either our primary or secondary calling. In many of the ways we're called to bless others, God doesn't want "the right hand to know what the left hand is doing." We aren't supposed to be in it for the applause. God, who sees what is done in secret, will reward you for everything you do in service to him, especially those things nobody else knows about (Matthew 6:4).

And speaking of little applause, the most important place we must share our unique calling is within our immediate family. If our primary calling is to be disciples who disciple others where we are, as Wilson says, then there is no greater opportunity for this kind of discipleship than in our own homes. We are certainly called to use our gifts and abilities to bless those closest to us. Nothing is more meaningful (where you're the *means* to their end) than being the most devoted and faithful husband, wife, dad, mom, son, or daughter possible. No other calling outside your home will be more challenging or rewarding.

Beyond our family, when we start seeing opportunities, we must be careful to filter them through the God-given purpose we're working hard to discover. One trap some people (like me) fall into, is that if someone is asking me to do something, I think their request must be my calling. Sensitive people like us have a hard time using the ancient word—"no." We naturally want to please people, so we become confused about our purpose because we're so busy accepting every opportunity to help.

Zig Ziglar helps with this problem, saying, "Opportunities are not synonymous with calling. There are more opportunities in life than any of us could possibly take advantage of. And many people never find their true calling in life because they don't measure opportunities against purpose."[176] That's another reason why it's so important to take the time to discover your calling. You'll be able to say "no" and "yes" to the right opportunities as they flow through the filter of your God-given purpose. If you do too much, you'll do nothing well, and will likely take important work away from someone else. (As with most of this book, I'm writing this to myself as well to as you.)

On the other hand, some people are so consumed with their own lives they don't have time to think about doing anything outside of their activities. If you (or your kids) have scheduled activities until late every night of the week and have no margin to be interrupted by God, you are missing out. Certainly there are seasons of crisis where a health challenge or job loss might keep you completely self-focused. In those times, your purpose is just to do your best and ask God and others to help you. But if the general course of your life is to be so filled with self-focused activity that you never serve in your church or community or neighborhood, you're missing a vital part of your calling. If that's you, I encourage you to free up your schedule and invite God to use you.

Just one more motive-related challenge: we are all called to do dirty work sometimes. A person who is called as a leader or a designer or a fair-trade coffee roaster still needs to clean toilets and take out the trash once in a while. The priest and the Levite who ignored the brutalized man on the street because of their "higher calling" missed the point. Only the Good Samaritan fulfilled his purpose that day (Luke 10:30-37). When there's a desperate need right in front of us, we are most definitely called by God to make a difference.

Motivated by The Call

Do you sense your calling? Do you know that God has something for you to do? Are you becoming aware of the ways you may be able to meet important needs like no one else?

If you don't sense it yet, something must be getting in the way. There's no doubt that God has called you. He has prepared good things for you to do, specifically at this time and place (Ephesians 2:10). You are "fearfully and wonderfully made" (Psalm 139:14). Jesus calls all of us to follow him (Mark 1:17). The testimony of the Scriptures is unanimous—you *are* made for a purpose.

There is an epic battle fighting to keep you from knowing and living out your God-given purpose. A world drowning in screens may be the most effective way in the history of mankind to keep people from hearing God's call. Zig Ziglar nailed it when he said, "Most of us have so many distractions, and in some cases so much baggage, that we plow through life unaware of the times when purpose and passion meet and create a broad boulevard named Calling. But I encourage you to begin looking for that crossroads—the place where purpose, passion, and peak performance meet—in your life for His glory and the deep gladness of your own heart."[177]

There is something unique that only you can share with this hurting world, and you'll only find it when you take the time to pursue it with all your heart. It's worth turning off every screen until you figure out what you're here to do. How tragic it would be to live your whole life without discovering and experiencing your purpose.

If you have a sense of purpose but don't know what it is, please take the time to read books like *More* and *The Purpose Driven Life*. It will take time and hard work, but nothing will fulfill you more than making a positive impact on your family and many others. As Todd Wilson says, "God is calling. And when you answer, this world will never be the same."[178]

Ultimately, God's will *will* be done on earth as it is in Heaven. But whether we participate to our full potential as part of God's plan is up to us. We have to be surrendered, free, renewed, available, and seeking. We have to be ready. "For the eyes of the LORD move to and fro throughout the earth that He may strongly support those whose heart is completely His" (2 Chronicles 16:9). He's looking for people who, like Isaiah, say, "Here am I, send me!" (Isaiah 6:8).

Thankfully, God's mercies "are new every morning" (Lamentations 3:23). We will never pursue our calling perfectly, nor does God expect us to. I've wasted years in fruitless pursuits, lost in temptations, trials, and self-focus. But by God's grace and goodness, I've learned these practices and am able pursue my calling more than ever in my life.

And I want this for you. I want to see you doing what you're here to do. Nothing would reward me more for writing this book than to hear how you are applying these biblical practices in your life and are able to live out your calling like never before. When you find yourself in that place, please email me at doug@thatdougsmith.com and tell me about it.

In our screen-saturated world, we need a movement of whole-heartedly committed Christ-followers who are willing to live in a counter-cultural way to address the urgent needs around us. As the world becomes more unstable and divided every day, real improvements aren't coming from the distracted masses. The only true solutions come from our Creator, who fills his willingly intentional followers with wisdom, grace, truth, and love to positively impact our broken world.

CHAPTER 12

[UN]INTENTIONAL

A COMMISSION FOR YOUR INTENTIONAL LIFE

Your Appointed Challenge

Alone, exhausted, and despairing, Frodo scales the treacherous mountain. He escaped the spider's cave and threw Gollum off a cliff, but the months of struggle to destroy the One Ring have nearly broken him. The power of the menacing dark lord and the crushing burden nearly overwhelms the hobbit, but Frodo perseveres. One foot in front of the other, clinging to cliff walls for stability, he plods forward, gasping for breath, until—

Whomp! Frodo falls flat on his face in utter exhaustion. But what is this? Warm light, beautiful trees, and green grass have appeared where sharp black rocks and gloom were just a moment ago. He then sees hope personified—the glowing, angelic beauty of Galadriel, queen of the elves. With an encouraging smile and an extended hand, she implores the ring-bearer to keep going.

"This task was appointed to you, Frodo of the Shire. If you do not find a way, no one will."

You aren't in the same place as Frodo—with the fate of the entire world depending on your ability to persevere and complete a nearly impossible quest. But someone's world does depend on something only you can do. There are people only you can reach, problems only you can solve, and needs only you can meet, by the grace and power of God. You *must* find and live in intentional freedom in Christ, and use your freedom to make a desperately needed difference in the world.

But living in a positive, counter-cultural way may seem as impossible as Frodo's task to destroy the Ring. Literally everywhere we look, we see family, friends, neighbors, and strangers who are all so immersed in technology they can't think of much else. Many millions of people are distracted, addicted, or obsessed. In a world filled with billions of devices and with billions more being made every year, what can one person do? What difference can we really make?

On our own, not much. But we serve the Creator of everything, the One who enjoys doing surprising miracles through small groups of people against overwhelming odds. By God's power, Gideon overthrew hordes of Midianite raiders with just 300 of his water-lapping friends. Eleven former cowards, discipled by Christ and empowered by the Holy Spirit, changed an entirely pagan Roman world. God is not limited.

Living in faithful surrender to God has always been less than popular. It's always been easier to go along with the self-focused crowd. But when the flow of culture is leading more and more people in the opposite direction of God's way, those who would follow him must become more intentional than ever. These surrendered Christ-followers will end up looking quite different from the media-saturated masses.

Free to Be Different

Jeremiah the prophet lived in a time like ours, and had a terribly difficult job. God commanded him to bring a very unpopular message to an idolatrous nation who didn't want to hear it. Every time Jeremiah shared God's latest post, the ancient versions of Reddit and Twitter would go nuts with backlash. They persecuted him for telling the truth, even throwing him into a well to try and silence him.

But God, because of his love, kept sending Jeremiah out with more unpopular posts, even though the people continually unfriended him. The message was that if the people kept up with their evil practices— like burning their children as sacrifices to false gods—then God would allow them to be taken captive by the Babylonians. Their country and entire way of life would be lost. This was God's gracious way of putting their self-destructiveness to a decisive end.

In the middle of Jeremiah's repeated warnings to the people, God asked Jeremiah to do something strange. He said, "Go to the house of the Rechabites and speak to them, and bring them into the house of the LORD, into one of the chambers, and give them wine to drink" (Jeremiah 35:2). The Rechabites were a devoted group of outsiders, not apparently part of the main Israelite community, but who were so devoted to God that the Bible hails them as scribes—important religious leaders (1 Chronicles 2:55).[179]

So God tells Jeremiah to test the Rechabites by bringing them into the temple and offering them pitchers of wine. These sons of Rechab fiercely resist, saying,

> We will not drink wine, for Jonadab the son of Rechab, our father, commanded us, saying, 'You shall not drink wine, you or your sons, forever. You shall not build a house, and you shall not sow seed and you shall not plant a vineyard or own one; but in tents you shall dwell all your days, that you may live many days in the land where you sojourn.' We have obeyed the voice of Jonadab the son of Rechab (JEREMIAH 35:6–8).

These Rechabites were different. Not only did they abstain from wine, but they didn't live in houses, didn't build businesses, and didn't do nearly anything the trendy, hip, cool, fast-paced and idol worshiping culture around them did. They must have seemed like the Amish to the rest of the country—strangely devoted to their way of life, and ridiculed by the majority as hopelessly out of touch.

Since the Rechabites passed the test by not drinking the wine, God used them as an object lesson for the rest of the wayward culture.

> Thus says the LORD of hosts, the God of Israel, 'Go and say to the men of Judah and the inhabitants of Jerusalem, "Will you not receive instruction by listening to My words?" declares the LORD. "The words of Jonadab the son of Rechab, which he commanded his sons not to drink

wine, are observed. So they do not drink wine to this day, for they have obeyed their father's command. But I have spoken to you again and again; yet you have not listened to Me. Also I have sent to you all My servants the prophets, sending them again and again, saying: 'Turn now every man from his evil way and amend your deeds, and do not go after other gods to worship them. Then you will dwell in the land which I have given to you and to your forefathers; but you have not inclined your ear or listened to Me. Indeed, the sons of Jonadab the son of Rechab have observed the command of their father which he commanded them, but this people has not listened to Me'"'
(JEREMIAH 35:13–16).

This story has important parallels for all of us who want to live a counter-culturally intentional life. *We can't keep living like the rest of our screen-obsessed society if we're going to follow God's ways in faithful freedom.* The desire-shaping power of our media environment is overwhelming without a decisive devotion to a different *way.* People who avoid desire-manipulating technologies may look as different in our time as the tent-dwelling teetotalers looked in Jeremiah's day when compared to those who were always partying in their affluent Israeli subdivisions.

I don't know what that difference looks like, exactly. It may be the subject of another book. But I do know this: unless we find and cast a positive vision for ourselves, our children, and our communities, we will be lost to distractions and addictions, unable to make a real Christ-centered difference in the world. We will waste the one life we have been given because we were so blinded by the media circus we couldn't see our neighbors enough to love them as ourselves.

We need a clearly defined ethos, something we can point to and say, "people like us do things like this, and here's why." It must be a message our kids can understand when we tell them why they can't have the same technology or access as other kids. I see it as a purpose-filled vision, like a creed or a mission statement they can embrace and even be proud of instead of feeling deprived.

Here's a suggested starting point for such a mission statement:

Recognizing the desire-shaping power of our modern screen-saturated age, we choose, intentionally, in surrendered obedience to Christ, to put high boundaries around our use of technology so that we can be free to know God and his ways, to hear his calling, obey his instructions, and become so filled with his love and wisdom that we are consistently available and empowered to make the biggest positive impact possible in this desperately needy world.

I encourage you to write your own statement of vision, one that resonates with your heart and inspires you and everyone around you to move purposely toward their intentional life.

Our calling from God needs to be so clear, our way of living as Christians needs to be so fully embraced, that the things we say "no" to aren't deprivations, but are simply unthinkable. They just don't fit with who we are and are becoming. Like a woman in her wedding dress would avoid playing in the mud and not feel deprived, we will avoid screen-manipulated desires without regret or remorse.

To reframe Galadriel: if Christians don't find a way to really live out the commands of Jesus Christ, even in today's world, no one will. If we don't find a way to build counter-cultural families and communities who support a different way of life than that which involves primarily self-focused screen immersion, no one will. If we aren't compelled by the needs of others around us to share God's love, justice, compassion, mercy, truth, and wisdom, no one will.

But by the grace of God, you and I will. We will wake up every morning in surrender, seeking with open hands and hearts to follow Christ. We will ask him to remove and renew and replace whatever he knows is best for us, even if it is uncomfortable. And we'll pursue the call to make a difference as God gives us the ability.

A Wonder-Full Life

One summer day while I was working on this book at the Brentwood, Tennessee library, a mom and her 9-year-old son were sitting at the next table. I could glance up at them over my laptop screen. The mom gave her son a notepad, pencil, and an eraser. He also had some kind of workbook. She sat next to him, quietly reading a paper book.

I was struck by the rare, almost quaint, yet somehow sacred scene. No devices. Her son wasn't clamoring for another video game. He sat still, thinking, writing, drawing—*creating*.

But this moved my heart even more. As I watched, the son's eyes wandered away from his notebook to the beautiful landscape visible through gorgeous wall-sized windows. There were lovely green trees, a brick courtyard with a large fountain, and excited birds clamoring for food. He looked out the window in wonder. *Wonder.* Mouth open, eyes wide. He was *in awe* of something he saw out there, so much so that he tapped his mom on the shoulder, and pointed it out to her.

What would he have missed if he had been staring at a screen? If he had been used to being on a screen all the time? Would he have missed the wonder of God's creation stirring in his heart? What if his mom was on her screen? Would she have missed the wonder too? Would she have missed giving her son the gift of a device-free morning, free to write on a notebook and think his own thoughts and learn and process and let his mind wander into the beauty of the outdoors?

My heart breaks for the millions of families who are missing this. The heavens declare the glory of God (Psalm 19:1). The trees of the field clap their hands (Isaiah 55:12). All creation declares the awesomeness of the God who made it (Romans 1:20). Most screens will tell you otherwise. They'll say God didn't create the world, is irrelevant, or that whatever is flashing on the screen right now is much more important than whatever God may or may not be doing.

When I lived in Idaho many years ago, my mentor Timothy used to take me up into the high mountain lakes to fish. These were very remote areas, with few people in sight. After driving for a couple hours and hiking a mile or two, we'd crest the high point and look down over picturesque mountain landscapes and pristine, blue water. We'd throw in our lines, and talk about the intersection of life and the Scriptures. We'd consider the depth and mysteries of God in the heart of his beautiful creation. I still treasure the *wonder* of those times.

Wonder creates a space for new possibilities. An expanse of potential where God's Spirit can intersect with our spirit in surprising and unexpected ways. In today's screen-saturated culture, only people with an intentional vision for their lives will make space for wonder. You can't wander into wonder. It takes intentionality.

Wonder is much more like an orchard of fruit trees than the produce aisle at the store. You can't just decide to run to the store to pick up a little wonder. You have to cultivate the ground, plant the trees, pull the weeds, fight the pests, water, and repeat. For a long time. Patiently. Sometimes without seeing any results or even knowing whether you'll get fruit for many years. But then, when you pick the fruit of your intentional life, you'll marvel at how wonder-full it is.

It's in times of wonder when you'll look up and clearly see God's artistry—not only in all of creation, but directly upon your life. You'll sense a renewed, wholehearted desire to join God in his mission to help as many people as possible find true freedom in Christ. And you'll see opportunities you never saw before to right wrongs, heal hurts, restore brokenness, and set captives free.

Your Intentional Life

Since you've stayed with me to the end, I know you're passionately seeking an intentional life. You care deeply about the state of the world, starting with your own life and family, all the way to today's global challenges. And you don't want to be filled with regret at the end of your life because you were unintentionally led astray from all the good God has for you to do.

Because of your diligence, you can look back over the chapter titles, and see how you're already seeing the [Un] begin to drop away from each character trait. You're more Aware, Prepared, Principled, Believing, Evaluating, Anticipating, Yielded, Changed, Transformed, Disciplined, Motivated, and yes, Intentional.

You've seen how God calls all of us to live an intentional life. Like me, you recognize how easily we can be pulled off-track by forces that are more intentional with our lives than we are. But you're done with that. You're already adopting biblical practices and are starting to see the potential for more freedom and impact than you may have known before.

I don't think you'll look at a screen—small or large—in the same way. I think you'll be like me when I drive by a school bus stop with kids all on their devices, sharing my heartsick feeling, wishing their parents could know what we've learned through this book. As for you and your house, things are going to be different, one intentional change at a time, by the grace and power of our kind and loving Heavenly Father.

In the middle of the book of Ephesians, Paul shares his heart for his friends through one of the most powerful prayers in the Bible. I've prayed this for my family for years, and it seems like a very fitting and inspiring passage to share as we come to the end of this time together. Though I don't know you, I'm praying this for you as I write.

> For this reason I bow my knees before the Father, from whom every family in heaven and on earth derives its name, that He would grant you, according to the riches of His glory, to be strengthened with power through His Spirit in the inner man, so that Christ may dwell in your hearts through faith; and that you, being rooted and grounded in love, may be able to comprehend with all the saints what is the breadth and length and height and depth, and to know the love of Christ which surpasses knowledge, that you may be filled up to all the fullness of God.
>
> Now to Him who is able to do far more abundantly beyond all that we ask or think, according to the power that works within us, to Him be the glory in the church and in Christ Jesus to all generations forever and ever. Amen (EPHESIANS 3:14–21).

May God fill you with his Spirit until you overflow, and may you see good fruit flourish in ways you can't even think of right now. I know it's possible, because even fifteen years ago I couldn't have imagined where God would take me as I was learning all I've shared with you. This book itself is just the latest and most concrete example of God's gracious work through my desire to live free in Christ. I trust God for even greater things in your life than you can ask or imagine as you follow him—intentionally.

■ ■ ■

If you'll join my email list at http://thatdougsmith.com, I'll keep you updated with the latest opportunities to connect with others who are embracing and living out their intentional life in our screen-saturated world. I also welcome your feedback, and would love to hear how these ideas are impacting you. Nothing would mean more to me than to know something in this book was helpful to you. Thank you!

[UN]ACKNOWLEDGED

A work of this scale, especially my first of this kind, is only possible because of the investment of a vast community of people who teach, support, encourage, and inspire. There are so many who have touched my life and enabled me to write and publish this book—way more than I'll be able to list here.

Tim Beals, thank you for believing in this project, for teaching this newbie the real world of the publishing process, and for assembling a perfectly suited team of professionals at Credo House Publishers to make this book what it needs to be "for such a time as this."

Michael Vander Klipp, thank you for pouring your whole heart and your masterful editing experience into refining the manuscript for publication. You instantly *got* my mission, and it showed in your incisive suggestions and your belief in the value of what I'm hoping to do through this book. You truly are a God-send.

Mick Silva, thank you for being the first publishing industry professional to say I had something here, even after only reading the ugly early drafts. You graciously gave me the warm and encouraging welcome into publishing I needed.

Bob Hostetler, thank you for your master class in book writing and for an incredibly valuable month of coaching. You showed a clueless novice how to crawl out from under my mountains of research to produce a book someone might actually want to read. Thank you for telling me, emphatically, to start over, when I didn't want to hear it. You are a direct and precise answer to prayer.

David Van Diest, thank you for believing in this project enough to lead me to write a solid proposal for you to pitch to the biggest houses in the industry, even though I was such a longshot. Your wisdom, experience, and depth of character, even under very challenging circumstances, inspired me and made this a much better work than it would have been. Plus, you did all that even after graduating from David Douglas High School. Amazing.

Dave Ramsey, thank you for agreeing to endorse this book, and for telling me you were proud of me. You taught me not only how to be a better money manager, but how to be a better man. I'm grateful beyond words for the time I had to watch you from the front row of your company. You modeled a mind-blowing vision of what is possible when relentless integrity, courage, and authentic faith are applied to the marketplace. Years of your infamous Wednesday devotionals made me believe this was possible.

Kevin Powell, thank you for being the only person besides Lyneta to walk step-by-step with me through every mountain and valley of this 2.5-year journey. You read every draft, and prayed earnestly with me every week. You are the very rare kind of friend, few in a lifetime, who can both tell me, "you nailed it" and, "you need to rewrite that chapter." You are a God-send; this wouldn't be half as effective without your vital contribution.

Dr. Timothy Barnett, thank you for seeing the value of this work, and for casting a vision of what may be possible. You took me under your wing over thirty years ago (!), and infused me with the unspeakably valuable gift of the knowledge that I could be a scholar without formal training if I'd just do the work. More importantly, you mentored me through every high and low of my adult life. You are truly "a friend who sticks closer than a brother." You inspire me by modeling intentionality at a super-human level in your own life, even under the most difficult circumstances.

Jim Ebert, thank you for being such a wonderful leader, for your faith, your example, and your encouragement. You inspire me to be a better man, husband, father, and disciple. You model the authentic, intentional, Christ-centered life.

For so many of my former Lampo teammates and leaders: I wanted to list you all, but after listing over thirty names I knew I'd forget someone. I appreciate every encouraging conversation, email, hug, smile, and the camaraderie of being connected with you on Dave's vital mission. So many of you *get* my mission too, and I'm so grateful for each of you.

Dan Banks, thank you for relentless enthusiasm, positivity, and for your powerful example what an "all-in" devotion to God looks like in family and in business. Your Christmas message to me hangs in my office as a constant reminder to "feed [his] sheep." May it be.

Lance Westbrooks, thank you for your prayers, accountability, and wise insight at critical parts of this process. Your friendship and the example of your life have blessed me more than I can say.

To the other men I meet with regularly: Bob Davis, thank you for saying, "it's working, and it's worth it" at a critical time. Joe McSorley, thank you for insightful critiques of early drafts and many prayers. Mark Morrison, thank you for your prayers, suggestions, and accountability.

Beta readers Stephanie Lockbaum (my firstborn), John Sloan, Roger Preston, Jen Casey, and Aaron West: thank you for your helpful and timely feedback. Thanks especially to Sloan for calling me, "Neo." That was over-the-top, but awesome.

Pastors Dr. Billy Grigory, Mark Bodenstab, Andy Hudelson, Dr. Bobby Harrington, and Josh Patrick: you taught, exhorted, discipled, and challenged me. Most of all, you modeled the reality of the gospel in your families in authentic and inspired ways. Thank you for investing so much in service of the King of kings. God has used you to shape me and my family profoundly.

Patti & Mark Foley, thank you for your countless prayers, encouragement, love, and vital mentoring over the years. You model a marriage, family, and devotion to God that I want when I grow up. You've adopted Lyneta and me into your family, being the parents Lyneta and I needed at critical times.

Don & Sharon Smith, Pop & Mom, thank you for teaching me perseverance, character and integrity, even as you endured the most grueling health challenges. You poured your whole lives into your kids, and I wouldn't be anything without your love, encouragement, and example. Losing you both was my Y2K crisis; but I know if you were still here, you'd tell me you were proud of me.

Lyneta, thank you for so much more than I can say. You read and edited every word of every draft for years, and filled your expert guidance with grace and truth. More than that, you walked closer with me through this than anyone. You believed in me when I didn't believe in myself, and you were willing to leap "off the cucumber" with me into only God knows where. You shared your decades of writing experience and wisdom, and even dragged me to my first life-changing writing conference. You're my best friend and sweetheart, my partner and my wife. None of this would have happened without you. I thank God for bringing us together, and I love you with all my heart. JOMK.

Finally, to our gracious God and our Lord Jesus Christ, thank you for being the source, the destination, and the reason for anything good contained in this book. I am nothing without you, but with you, I can do immeasurably more than I can ask or imagine. Thank you for calling me as a lost, foolish young man, and by your gracious work in every area of my life—even through my many failings and wrong turns—for leading me to the place where I have something of value to offer. You have given me everything needed for each step along the way, often in inexplicably miraculous ways. I offer this work, and my life, once again, in surrender to you alone, and trust you'll use it all for your good purposes.

ENDNOTES

1   eMarketer Staff (no author listed), "US Adults Now Spend 12 Hours 7 Minutes a Day Consuming Media," *eMarketer:* https://www.emarketer.com/Article/US-Adults-Now-Spend-12-Hours-7-Minutes-Day-Consuming-Media/1015775 (May 1, 2017)

2   eMarketer Staff (no author listed), "Average Time Spent per Day with Major Media by US Adults, 2012-2018," *eMarketer:* https://www.emarketer.com/Chart/Average-Time-Spent-per-Day-with-Major-Media-by-US-Adults-2012-2018-hrsmins/188929 (April 18, 2016)

3   Ron Marshall, "How Many Ads Do You See in One Day?" *Red Crow Marketing:* http://www.redcrowmarketing.com/2015/09/10/many-ads-see-one-day/ (September 10, 2015)

4   Barry Ritholtz, "Data Never Sleeps," *The Big Picture:* http://ritholtz.com/2017/05/data-never-sleeps-2 (May 5, 2017)

5   Alex Hern, "Netflix's biggest competitor? Sleep," *The Guardian:* https://www.theguardian.com/technology/2017/apr/18/netflix-competitor-sleep-uber-facebook (April 18, 2017)

6   Madlen Davies, "Average person now spends more time on their phone and laptop than SLEEPING, study claims," *DailyMail.com:* http://www.dailymail.co.uk/health/article-2989952/How-technology-taking-lives-spend-time-phones-laptops-SLEEPING.html (March 11, 2015)

7   Jim VandeHei, Sara Fischer, "How tech ate the media and our minds," *Axios:* https://www.axios.com/searching-for-information-nirvana-2248588151.html (Feb 10, 2017)

8   Horace Dediu, "The most popular product of all time," *Asymco:* http://www.asymco.com/2016/07/28/most-popular-product-of-all-time/ (July 28, 2016)

9   Denis Campbell, "Facebook and Twitter 'harm young people's mental health'," *The Guardian:* https://www.theguardian.com/society/2017/may/19/popular-social-media-sites-harm-young-peoples-mental-health (May 19, 2017)

10   Fight The New Drug Staff (no author listed), "What's The Average Age Of Someone's First Exposure To Porn?" *Fight The New Drug:* https://fightthenewdrug.org/real-average-age-of-first-exposure/ (August 10, 2017)

11   Dr. Nicholas Kardaras, "Screens in Schools are a $60 Billion Hoax," *Time:* http://time.com/4474496/screens-schools-hoax/ (August 31, 2016)

12   Dr. Nicholas Kardaras, "Screens in Schools are a $60 Billion Hoax," *Time:* http://time.com/4474496/screens-schools-hoax/ (August 31, 2016)

13   Perri Klass, M.D., "Fixated by Screens, but Seemingly Nothing Else," *The New York Times:* http://www.nytimes.com/2011/05/10/health/views/10klass.html (May 9, 2011)

14   Dave Mosher, "High Wired: Does Addictive Internet Use Restructure the Brain?" *Scientific American:* http://www.scientificamerican.com/article/does-addictive-internet-use-restructure-brain/ (June 17, 2011)

15   ISU News Staff (no author listed), "ISU study proves conclusively that violent video game play makes more aggressive kids," *Iowa State University News Service:* http://www.news .iastate.edu/news/2010/mar/vvgeffects (March 1, 2010)

16   Andrew Careaga, "Internet usage patterns may signify depression," *Missouri University of Science and Technology:* http://news.mst.edu/2012/05/internet_usage_patterns_may_ si/ (May 22, 2012)

17   Arden D. Dingle, M.D., Jay S. Kothari, M.D., "Psychiatric Impacts of Video Games, Internet Addiction on Children," *Psychiatry Advisor:* http://www.psychiatryadvisor.com/ childadolescent-psychiatry/psychiatric-impacts-of-video-games-internet-addiction-on -children/article/396984/ (February 06, 2015)

18   Angelica B. Ortiz de Gortari & Mark D. Griffiths, "Prevalence and Characteristics of Game Transfer Phenomena: A Descriptive Survey Study," *Taylor & Francis Group:* http:// www.tandfonline.com/doi/abs/10.1080/10447318.2016.1164430 (March 16, 2016)

19   Joe Clement, *Screen Schooled: Two Veteran Teachers Expose How Technology Overuse Is Making Our Kids Dumber,* First Kindle Edition (Chicago Review Press, 2018), 22.

20   Katie Mettler, "Smartphones made his kids 'moody' and 'withdrawn.' Now he wants to ban them for preteens," *The Washington Post:* https://www.washingtonpost.com/news/ morning-mix/wp/2017/06/19/why-a-colorado-dad-is-fighting-to-make-smartphones -for-preteens-illegal/ (June 19, 2017)

21   Doug Smith, *ThatDougSmith.com:* https://thatdougsmith.com/category/free-will/

22   Simon Sinek, "Simon Sinek on Millennials in the Workplace," *YouTube:* https://www .youtube.com/watch?v=hER0Qp6QJNU (October 29, 2016)
     David Gosse, "Transcript of Simon Sinek Millennials in the Workplace Interview," *Ochen:* http://ochen.com/transcript-of-simon-sineks-millennials-in-the-workplace -interview (January 4, 2017)

23   Saul McLeod, "Pavlov's Dogs," *Simply Psychology:* http://www.simplypsychology.org/ pavlov.html (2013)

24   Seth Godin, "Pavlov's in your pocket," *Seth's Blog:* http://sethgodin.typepad.com/seths_ blog/2017/01/pavlovs-in-your-pocket.html (January 15, 2017)

25   Adam Alter, *Irresistible: The Rise of Addictive Technology and the Business of Keeping Us Hooked,* Kindle Edition (New York: Penguin Publishing Group, 2017), 70–71.

26   Adam Alter, *Irresistible,* 72.

27   Adam Alter, *Irresistible,* 87.

28   Adam Alter, *Irresistible,* 72. Emphasis mine.

29   Adam Alter, *Irresistible,* 5.

30   Nir Eyal, "How To Manufacture Desire," *TechCrunch:* https://techcrunch.com/2012/03/ 04/how-to-manufacture-desire/ (March 4, 2012)

31   Delaney Ruston, *ScreenagersMovie:* https://screenagersmovie.com

32   Ian Leslie, "The Scientists Who Make Apps Addictive," *1843 Magazine:* https:// www.1843magazine.com/features/the-scientists-who-make-apps-addictive (October/ November 2016)

33   Chris Nodder, *Evil by Design: Interaction Design to Lead Us into Temptation,* Kindle Edition (New York: Wiley, 2013), location 147.

34   Chris Nodder, *Evil by Design,* locations 132–133.

35   Chris Nodder, *Evil By Design:* http://evilbydesign.info/

36   Chris Nodder, "Impatience Leads to Compliance," *Evil By Design:* http://evilbydesign .info/gluttony/impatience-leads-to-compliance/

37   Chris Nodder, "The Path of Least Resistance," *Evil By Design:* http://evilbydesign.info/sloth/path-of-least-resistance/

38   Wikipedia, "Golden Age of Television (2000s–present)," *Wikipedia:* https://en.wikipedia.org/wiki/Golden_Age_of_Television_(2000s–present) (Last edited July 1 2018)

39   Neil Postman, *Amusing Ourselves To Death: Public Discourse in the Age of Show Business,* New Edition w/Introduction by Andrew Postman (New York: Penguin Books, 2006), 127.

40   Michael Moss, "The Extraordinary Science of Addictive Junk Food," *The New York Times Magazine:* http://www.nytimes.com/2013/02/24/magazine/the-extraordinary-science-of-junk-food.html (February 20, 2013)

41   Neil Postman, *Amusing Ourselves To Death,* 128.

42   Neil Postman, *Amusing Ourselves To Death,* 128.

43   Neil Postman, *Amusing Ourselves To Death,* 131.

44   Neil Postman, *Amusing Ourselves To Death,* 155–156.

45   David Heinemeier Hansson (DHH), "The price of monetizing schemes," *Medium:* https://m.signalvnoise.com/the-price-of-monetizing-schemes-454141dab027 (January 13, 2017)

46   Katharine Schwab, "Nest Founder: "I Wake Up In Cold Sweats Thinking, What Did We Bring To The World?" *Fast Company:* https://www.fastcodesign.com/90132364/nest-founder-i-wake-up-in-cold-sweats-thinking-what-did-we-bring-to-the-world (July 7, 2017)

47   Katharine Schwab, "Nest Founder: "I Wake Up In Cold Sweats Thinking, What Did We Bring To The World?" *Fast Company:* https://www.fastcodesign.com/90132364/nest-founder-i-wake-up-in-cold-sweats-thinking-what-did-we-bring-to-the-world (July 7, 2017)

48   Adam Alter, *Irresistible,* 1.

49   Adam Alter, *Irresistible,* 2.

50   Jeff Desjardins, "Chart: The Largest Companies by Market Cap Over 15 Years," *Visual Capitalist:* http://www.visualcapitalist.com/chart-largest-companies-market-cap-15-years/ (August 12, 2016)

51   Scott Galloway, *The Four: The Hidden DNA of Amazon, Apple, Facebook, and Google,* Kindle Edition (New York, Penguin Publishing, 2017), 2.

52   Scott Galloway, *The Four,* 4.

53   Scott Galloway, *The Four,* 3–4.

54   Scott Galloway, *The Four,* 134.

55   Jeff Desjardins, "Chart: Here's How 5 Tech Giants Make Their Billions," *Visual Capitalist:* http://www.visualcapitalist.com/chart-5-tech-giants-make-billions/ (May 12, 2017)

56   Scott Galloway, *The Four,* 9.

57   DHH is David Heinemeier Hansson, inventor of the industry-shaping web development framework Ruby on Rails, and a partner at Basecamp.

58   David Heinemeier Hansson (DHH), "Exponential growth devours and corrupts," *Medium:* https://m.signalvnoise.com/exponential-growth-devours-and-corrupts-c5562fbf131 (February 27, 2017) This is a really important article, worth reading and pondering.

59   David Heinemeier Hansson (DHH), "Exponential growth devours and corrupts," *Medium:* https://m.signalvnoise.com/exponential-growth-devours-and-corrupts-c5562fbf131 (February 27, 2017)

60   Marc Andreessen, "Why Software Is Eating the World," *Andreessen Horowitz:* https://a16z.com/2016/08/20/why-software-is-eating-the-world/ (Originally published in the Wall Street Journal on August 20, 2011) Andreessen, founder of Netscape, was optimistic when he said, "software is eating the world." He's right, but I don't think it's nearly as rosy as he thought then.

61   Neal Larson & Rebecca Adams, *Living in Spin: How Media Gurus and PR Czars Open our Wallets and Scramble our Logic,* Kindle Edition (Neven Media, 2006), 13.

62   Neal Larson & Rebecca Adams, *Living in Spin,* 32.

63   Edward Bernays, *Propaganda,* Kindle Edition (Brooklyn: Ig Publishing, 2005, originally published by Bernays in 1928), 1.

64   Edward Bernays, *Propaganda,* 1 (in 1928, the U.S. population was near 120 million).

65   Edward Bernays, *Propaganda,* 2–3. Emphasis mine.

66   Aldous Huxley, "1961: Aldous Huxley's eerie prediction at Tavistock Group, California Medical School," Quoted on the site of *Alliance for Human Research Protection (AHRP):* http://ahrp.org/1961-aldous-huxleys-eerie-prediction-at-tavistock-group-california-medical-school/ (1961). Emphasis mine.

67   Mark Zuckerberg, "Bringing the World Closer Together," *Facebook:* https://www.facebook.com/zuck/posts/10154944663901634 (June 22, 2017)

68   Mark Zuckerberg, "Bringing the World Closer Together," *Facebook:* https://www.facebook.com/zuck/posts/10154944663901634 (June 22, 2017)

69   "Mark Zuckerberg's Commencement address at Harvard," *The Harvard Gazette:* https://news.harvard.edu/gazette/story/2017/05/mark-zuckerbergs-speech-as-written-for-harvards-class-of-2017/ (May 25, 2017)

70   "Mark Zuckerberg's Commencement address at Harvard," *The Harvard Gazette:* https://news.harvard.edu/gazette/story/2017/05/mark-zuckerbergs-speech-as-written-for-harvards-class-of-2017/ (May 25, 2017)

71   Scott Galloway, "Amazon Takes Over the World," *The Wall street Journal:* https://www.wsj.com/articles/amazon-takes-over-the-world-1506104228 (Sept 22, 2017)

72   Many articles talk about Amazon's destruction of retail, including: Steve Dennis, "Assessing The Damage Of 'The Amazon Effect," *Forbes:* https://www.forbes.com/sites/stevendennis/2017/06/19/should-we-care-whether-amazon-is-systematically-destroying-retail/ (June 19, 2017). Amazon's "bruising" and stressful working conditions were documented by the New York Times and others: Jodi Kantor & David Streitfeld, "Inside Amazon: Wrestling Big Ideas in a Bruising Workplace," *The New York Times:* https://www.nytimes.com/2015/08/16/technology/inside-amazon-wrestling-big-ideas-in-a-bruising-workplace.html (August 15, 2015. Galloway's book goes into a lot more detail on economy-destroying practices of The Four.

73   Kate Vinton, "Jeff Bezos Overtakes Bill Gates To Become World's Richest Man," *Forbes:* https://www.forbes.com/sites/katevinton/2017/07/27/jeff-bezos-overtakes-bill-gates-to-become-worlds-richest-man (July 27, 2017)

74   Danielle Wiener-Bronner, "Mark Zuckerberg is now the third-richest person alive," *CNN:* https://money.cnn.com/2018/07/06/technology/business/mark-zuckerberg-warren-buffett/index.html (July 6, 2018)

75   Many of our angry feelings are manufactured by social media-fueled propaganda. In an article in *New York Magazine* titled, "An Apology for the Internet," early Facebook investor Roger McNamee tattles on the industry, and even connects current trends with Edward Bernays (in case you doubted my use of the word *propaganda*):

      "They're basically trying to trigger fear and anger to get the outrage cycle going, because outrage is what makes you more deeply engaged. You spend more time on the site and you share more stuff. Therefore, you're going to be exposed to more ads, and that makes you more valuable. In 2008, when [Facebook] put their first app on the iPhone, the whole ballgame changed. **Suddenly Bernays's dream of the universal platform reaching everybody through every medium at the same time was achieved by a single device**. You marry the social triggers to personalized content on a device that most people check on their way to pee in the morning and as the last thing they do before they turn the light out at night. **You literally have a persuasion engine unlike any created in history."***

Isn't that—outrageous? The elites behind our screens *know* and *tell* how they are manipulating the world with an "outrage cycle." The angrier they make us, the more we "engage" with their apps. And while they squeeze billions of dollars out of our angry attention, we are left irrationally divided, unable to have a reasonable discussion. And the mobs formed by manufactured outrage do real damage.

* Noah Kulwin, "An Apology for the Internet from the People Who Built It," *New York Magazine:* http://nymag.com/selectall/2018/04/an-apology-for-the-internet-from -the-people-who-built-it.html (April 13, 2018). Emphasis mine. A long and important article—especially the Roger McNamee quotes.

76 Scott Galloway, *The Four*, 266.

77 Scott Galloway, *The Four*, 268. Emphasis mine.

78 David Heinemeier Hansson (DHH), "Exponential growth devours and corrupts," *Medium:* https://m.signalvnoise.com/exponential-growth-devours-and-corrupts-c5562fbf131 (February 27, 2017)

79 Anjelica Oswald, "The top TV show from every year since 1967," *Business Insider:* http://www.businessinsider.com/best-tv-shows-ever-2017-8/#1967-the-andy-griffith-show-1 (August 12, 2017)

80 Noah Filipiak, "If you are watching "Game of Thrones," you are watching porn," *Covenant Eyes:* http://www.covenanteyes.com/2016/02/02/if-you-are-watching-game -of-thrones-you-are-watching-porn/ (February 2, 2016)

81 Kyle Buchanan, "This Is Why Game of Thrones Has So Much Nudity," *Vulture:* http://www.vulture.com/2012/06/game-of-thrones-nudity-nude-scenes.html (June 4, 2012)

82 Fox News Staff, "10 memorable quotes from Playboy founder Hugh Hefner," *Fox News:* http://www.foxnews.com/entertainment/2017/09/28/10-memorable-quotes-from -playboy-founder-hugh-hefner.html (September 28, 2017)

83 A reference to the musical *My Fair Lady*, where a poor woman of the street is acculturated by the grueling coaching of a professor to pass for a high-society princess.

84 Read Mercer Schuchardt, "Hugh Hefner's Hollow Victory: How the Playboy magnate won the culture war, lost his soul, and left us with a mess to clean up," *Christianity Today:* http://www.christianitytoday.com/ct/2003/december/hugh-hefners-hollow -victory.html (December 1, 2003). Another very important article, worth your time.

85 "Free Speech Coalition," *Wikipedia:* https://en.wikipedia.org/wiki/Free_Speech_ Coalition (Last edited: July 1, 2018)

86 Dan Hewitt, "U.S. Video Game Industry Generates $30.4 Billion in Revenue for 2016," *BusinessWire:* http://www.businesswire.com/news/home/20170119005313/en/U.S. -Video-Game-Industry-Generates-30.4-Billion (January 19, 2017)

87 Jennifer M. Proffitt, Ph.D. and Margot A. Susca, Ph.D., "Follow the Money: The Entertainment Software Association Attack on Video Game Regulation," *Academia:* https://www.academia.edu/2021684/Follow_the_Money_The_Entertainment_ Software_Association_Attack_on_Video_Game_Regulation

88 Jennifer M. Proffitt & Margot A. Susca, "Follow the Money," 24–25.

89 John Stonestreet, "BreakPoint: Numbed by Video Games," *BreakPoint:* http://www .breakpoint.org/2017/06/breakpoint-numbed-by-video-games/ (June 26, 2017). Emphasis mine.

90 "The Lord of the Rings: Fellowship of the Ring, The Script at IMSDb," *IMSDB:* http://www .imsdb.com/scripts/Lord-of-the-Rings-Fellowship-of-the-Ring,-The.html

91   "The Lord of the Rings: Fellowship of the Ring, The Script at IMSDb," *IMSDB:* http://www .imsdb.com/scripts/Lord-of-the-Rings-Fellowship-of-the-Ring,-The.html

92   "The Lord of the Rings: Fellowship of the Ring, The Script at IMSDb," *IMSDB:* http://www .imsdb.com/scripts/Lord-of-the-Rings-Fellowship-of-the-Ring,-The.html

93   Richard Dawkins, "Quotable Quote," *Goodreads:* https://www.goodreads.com/ quotes/4416-we-are-all-atheists-about-most-of-the-gods-that

94   If you're interested in more about the reliability of the Bible, there are a ton of excellent resources. I wrote a blog post linking to several of them here: https://www.afterlife .co.nz/2013/01/why-care-about-the-bible-and-what-it-says/.

95   CDC Staff, "Ten Leading Causes of Death and Injury," *Centers for Disease Control and Prevention:* https://www.cdc.gov/injury/wisqars/leadingcauses.html (2016 stats)

96   Jean M. Twenge, "Have Smartphones Destroyed a Generation?" *The Atlantic:* https:// www.theatlantic.com/magazine/archive/2017/09/has-the-smartphone-destroyed-a -generation/534198/ (September 2017 Issue). A pivotal article, widely cited.

97   Billboard staff, "The Hot 100," *Billboard:* https://www.billboard.com/charts/hot-100/ 1977-12-16 (December 17, 1977)

98   Billboard staff, "The Hot 100," *Billboard:* https://www.billboard.com/charts/hot-100/ 2017-12-16 (December 17, 2017)

99   Debbie Boone / Kasey Cisyk, "You Light Up My Life," *AZ Lyrics:* https://www.azlyrics.com/ lyrics/debbyboone/youlightupmylife.html

100   Post Malone, "Rockstar," *AZ Lyrics:* https://www.azlyrics.com/lyrics/postmalone/ rockstar.html

101   Os Guinness, *Impossible People: Christian Courage and the Struggle for the Soul of Civilization,* Kindle Edition (Downers Grove, IL: InterVarsity Press, 2016), Kindle locations 1208–1214.

102   Os Guinness, *Impossible People,* Kindle locations 2891–2899.

103   C. S. Lewis, *The Screwtape Letters,* HarperCollins Edition (San Francisco: HarperCollins, 2001, original copyright 1942), 31–32.

104   John Wesley, "Sermons On Several Occasions - Sermon 72: Of Evil Angels," *Christian Classics Ethereal Library:* http://www.ccel.org/ccel/wesley/sermons.vi.xix.html (1771)

105   John Wesley, "Sermon 72: Of Evil Angels"

106   Amy B. Wang, "'Post-truth' named 2016 word of the year by Oxford Dictionaries," *The Washington Post:* https://www.washingtonpost.com/news/the-fix/wp/2016/11/16/post -truth-named-2016-word-of-the-year-by-oxford-dictionaries/ (November 16, 2016)

107   Albert Barnes, "Notes from the Bible," *BibleHub:* http://biblehub.com/commentaries/ 2_corinthians/4-4.htm (1834)

108   Albert Barnes, "Notes from the Bible," *BibleHub:* http://biblehub.com/commentaries/ 2_corinthians/4-4.htm (1834)

109   Os Guinness, *Impossible People,* Kindle locations 1276–1284. Emphasis mine.

110   Samuel Taylor Coleridge, *Aids to Reflection and the Confessions of an Inquiring Spirit,* Project Gutenberg eBook edition (London: George Bell and Sons, 1884), Kindle location 186.

111   Dr. Kimberly Young, "What you need to know about internet addiction (TEDxBuffalo)," *YouTube:* https://www.youtube.com/watch?v=vOSYmLER664 (January 5, 2015)

112   Matthew Kelly, *Perfectly Yourself: 9 Lessons for Enduring Happiness,* Second Edition (North Palm Beach, FL: Beacon Publishing, 2006), Kindle locations 734–735.

113   Matthew Kelly, *Perfectly Yourself,* 465–466.

114   Rod Dreher, "The Walker Percy Option," *The American Conservative:* http://www
       .theamericanconservative.com/dreher/the-walker-percy-option/ (February 7, 2018)

115   Jean M. Twenge, "Have Smartphones Destroyed a Generation?" *The Atlantic:* https://
       www.theatlantic.com/magazine/archive/2017/09/has-the-smartphone-destroyed-a
       -generation/534198/ (September 2017 Issue).

116   See Families Managing Media's research on the harmful effects of screens on
       developing young brains. http://www.familiesmanagingmedia.com/blog/

117   Andy Andrews, *The Noticer*, Hardback Edition (Nashville: Thomas Nelson, 2009), 9.

118   Quoted from my blog, https://thatdougsmith.com/2017/12/03/remembering-a-hero-of
       -the-faith/, where I quoted Sara Faye's post here: https://edwardfudge.com/gracemail
       -november-26th-2017/. Edward Fudge is one of my heroes, someone who inspires my
       vision. Raised in a Christian home in Alabama in the 40's and 50's, he was inspired by
       his love for God and the Bible to become a Bible teacher, author, and later, an attorney.
       Most importantly, he was willing to challenge deeply held beliefs related to God's grace,
       racial harmony (in the South!), and conditional immortality. Edward's vision gave him
       amazing perseverance, all with a humble, gracious, and kind spirit. I've written more
       about Edward at http://thatdougsmith.com if you'd like more details about him, his
       writings, and even the movie that was made about his life.

119   Jeff Brown, "How to Leave a Legacy (A Tribute to My Father)," *The Read to Lead Podcast:*
       http://readtoleadpodcast.com/203 (February 19, 2018)

120   For the biblical practices chapters, I'm diverging from setting the tone with a movie
       scene, choosing to open instead with Bible verses and other quotes. If you liked the movie
       setups, you'll be glad to know there's one more to look forward to in the last chapter.

121   Dallas Willard, *The Great Omission Reclaiming Jesus's Essential Teachings on Discipleship,*
       ePub Edition (HarperCollins, 2006), Kindle Locations 1033-1034.

122   Ironically, as Spock aged, his character matured and broadened his perspective so much
       that in the movie *Star Trek 6: The Undiscovered Country* he asked a young protégé to
       "have faith."

123   Matthew Bates, *Salvation by Allegiance Alone*, Edition (Grand Rapids, MI: Baker
       Academic, 2017), 67. If you're looking for clarity around the general message of the
       Christian Gospel, this book is an outstanding, clear, and comprehensive presentation.

124   Os Guinness, *Impossible People: Christian Courage and the Struggle for the Soul of
       Civilization*, Kindle Edition (InterVarsity Press, 2017), Kindle Locations 883-884.

125   Gregory A. Boyd, *Present Perfect: Finding God in the Now*, Kindle Edition (Zondervan,
       2010), 48.

126   Greg Boyd, *Present Perfect*, p. 68.

127   Greg Boyd, *Present Perfect*, p. 75.

128   Greg Boyd, *Present Perfect*, p. 100. Emphasis mine.

129   Greg Boyd, *Present Perfect*, p. 71.

130   Greg Boyd, *Present Perfect*, p. 89.

131   Greg Boyd, *Present Perfect*, p. 48.

132   Neil T. Anderson, *The Bondage Breaker*, Kindle Edition (Harvest House Publishers,
       2006), 39.

133   Methodist Worship Book, page 290. © 1999 Trustees for Methodist Church Purposes,
       quoted from http://www.methodist.org.uk/about-us/the-methodist-church/what-is-
       distinctive-about-methodism/a-covenant-with-god/. The Methodist study guide on the
       prayer (https://www.rootsontheweb.com/content/PDFs/346041/Methodist_Covenant_
       Prayer_study.pdf) says that John Wesley introduced a version of this prayer in 1755,

pulling from prayers written by seventeenth-century Puritan divines Joseph and Richard Alleine.

134 Some inconclusive but interesting debate from Quote Investigator about the origin of this quote is here: https://quoteinvestigator.com/2016/04/25/get/.

135 Jean M. Twenge, "Tech bosses limit their kids' time on smartphones: why shouldn't we?," *The Guardian:* https://www.theguardian.com/commentisfree/2018/jan/12/tech-bosses-kids-time-smartphones-parents-mental-health (January 12, 2018)

136 Tim Challies, "Are You Godly Enough to Watch Smut?," *Tim Challies Blog:* https://www.challies.com/articles/are-you-godly-enough-to-watch-smut/ (March 21, 2018)

137 Melanie Hempe, "The Gates Family Agrees To Delay Smartphones for Kids," *Families Managing Media:* http://www.familiesmanagingmedia.com/gates-family-agrees-delay-smartphones-kids/ (October 13, 2017)

138 Melanie Hempe, "The Gates Family Agrees To Delay Smartphones for Kids"

139 https://www.covenanteyes.com

140 https://forcefield.me

141 https://meetcircle.com

142 Dr. Meg Meeker, "Is Your Phone Ruining Your Kids," *Meg Meeker MD:* https://megmeekermd.com/blog/is-your-phone-ruining-your-kids/ (October 4, 2016). Dr. Meg Meeker, "Teens and Social Media: Time to Dial it Down," *Meg Meeker MD:* https://megmeekermd.com/blog/teens-and-social-media-time-to-dial-it-down/ (November 21, 2017)

143 Quoted by Greg Boyd, *Present Perfect,* 87.

144 If you haven't witnessed the miraculous transformation of a caterpillar to a butterfly recently or in great detail, take an hour (after your finish this chapter, of course) and watch Illustra Media's *Metamorphosis: The Beauty and Design of Butterflies.* http://www.metamorphosisthefilm.com. It'll renew your mind in a beautiful way.

145 From reading Charles Finney years ago, I learned that the opposite of love is not hate, but is selfishness. Love, unlike what our culture teaches us, isn't about our sexual appetites at all. The Bible says "greater love has no one than this, that one lay down his life for his friends" (John 15). Finney calls love "disinterested benevolence," meaning choosing the highest good of God and others without regard for what is in it for us. It's a selfless choice of the good of everyone else. So, it's ultimately the opposite of selfishness.

146 As rendered in NIV. I usually prefer more literal Bibles, but they didn't translate Romans 12:2 as well as NIV in my view. ESV says, "so that you may discern what is the will of God" and NASB says, "so that you may prove what the will of God is." The NIV, a phrase-by-phrase instead of word-for-word translation, renders the fullness of this important phrase.

147 http://biblehub.com/greek/1381.htm

148 Sir Arthur Conan Doyle, "A Study In Scarlett," *The Complete Novels and Stories, Volume 1,* Edition (Bantam, 2003, first published 1887), 13. Emphasis mine.

149 Zig Ziglar, "Change What Goes Into Your Mind," *Ziglar.com:* https://www.ziglar.com/quotes/you-are-what-you-are-and-where-you-are/

150 Kenneth Boa, *Life in the Presence of God: Practices for Living in Light of Eternity,* Kindle Edition (InterVarsity Press, 2017), 35.

151 Charles G. Finney, *Finney's Systematic Theology,* New Expanded Edition (Minneapolis: Bethany House Publishers, 1994), 2.

152 Find Precept Ministries International at https://www.precept.org.

153 Luke Veldt, "Andrea," *Memorize Psalm 119:* http://memorizepsalm119.com/andrea/

154 Zig Ziglar, *Better Than Good,* (Nashville: Thomas Nelson, Inc., 2006), 119.

155 Matthew Kelly. *Perfectly Yourself,* Kindle Locations 907-913. (Emphasis mine)

156 Zig Ziglar, *Better Than Good,* 117.

157 Person Sprinkle, "Can you be porn free with an iPhone?" *Theology In The Raw Podcast:* https://www.prestonsprinkle.com/theology-in-the-raw/2017/10/9/allknsbspbrkficiq6412107qsllnf (October 9, 2017)

158 Charles Duhigg, *The Power of Habit: Why We Do What We Do in Life and Business,* Kindle Edition (Random House Publishing Group, 2014), 29.

159 Stephen Mansfield, "Habits and the Brain," *StephenMansfield.tv:* https://stephenmansfield.tv/habits-and-the-brain-2/ (July 12, 2017)

160 http://biblehub.com/hebrew/1870.htm

161 http://biblehub.com/greek/1838.htm

162 http://biblehub.com/greek/1128.htm

163 Kenneth Boa, *Life in the Presence of God: Practices for Living in Light of Eternity,* Kindle Edition (InterVarsity Press, 2017), 94.

164 Charles Duhigg, *The Power of Habit,* 84-85.

165 Cal Newport, "The Rise of the Monk Mode Morning," *CalNewport.com:* http://calnewport.com/blog/2017/02/24/the-rise-of-the-monk-mode-morning (February 24, 2017)

166 Matthew Kelly, *Perfectly Yourself: 9 Lessons for Enduring Happiness,* Kindle Edition (Beacon Publishing, 2006), Kindle Locations 907-913. (Emphasis mine.)

167 Todd Wilson, *More: Find Your Personal Calling and Live Life to the Fullest Measure,* Kindle Edition (Grand Rapids: Zondervan, 2016), 11.

168 Rick Warren, *The Purpose Driven® Life* (Grand Rapids: Zondervan, 2002), 17.

169 Andy Stanley, "The Complexity Of Purpose, Part 2," *The Andy Stanley Leadership Podcast:* https://andystanley.com/the-complexity-of-purpose-part-2/ (October 5, 2017)

170 Andy Stanley, "The Complexity Of Purpose, Part 2," *The Andy Stanley Leadership Podcast:* https://andystanley.com/the-complexity-of-purpose-part-2/ (October 5, 2017)

171 Todd Wilson, "Rick Warren Interview," *Find Your Calling Podcast:* https://toddwilson.org/find-your-calling-podcast/ (June 6, 2016)

172 Todd Wilson, *More,* 15.

173 Todd Wilson, *More,* 99.

174 Zig Ziglar, *Better than Good,* 161.

175 Todd Wilson, *More,* 90.

176 Zig Ziglar, *Better than Good,* 179.

177 Zig Ziglar, *Better than Good,* 186.

178 Todd Wilson, *More,* 11.

179 See more details about the Rechabites here: Executive Committee of the Editorial Board., George A. Barton, Wilhelm Bacher, Judah David Eisenstein, "Rechabites," *The Jewish Encyclopedia,* http://jewishencyclopedia.com/articles/12616-rechabites, originally published 1906.